Teaching Your Children Sensitivity

Linda & Richard Eyre

A FIRESIDE BOOK
Simon & Schuster
New York London Toronto
Sydney Tokyo Singapore

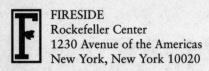

FIRESIDE
Rockefeller Center
1230 Avenue of the Americas
New York, New York 10020

Copyright © 1987 by R. M. Eyre and Assoc. Inc.
Revised Edition Copyright © 1995 by Richard Eyre and Linda Eyre

FIRESIDE and colophon are registered trademarks
of Simon & Schuster Inc.

Designed by Levavi & Levavi

Manufactured in the United States of America

10   9   8   7   6   5   4   3   2   1

Library of Congress Cataloging-in-Publication Data
Eyre, Linda
    Teaching your children sensitivity / Linda and Richard Eyre—
Rev. ed.
        p.   cm.
    "A Fireside book"
    Rev. ed. of: Teaching children sensitivity. 1st ed. New York:
Random House, 1988.
    Includes index.
    1. Empathy. 2. Empathy—Problems, exercises, etc. 3.Child
rearing. I. Eyre, Richard M. II. Eyre, Linda. Teaching children
sensitivity. III. Title.
BF575.E55E87   1995   94-37008
649' .7—dc20   CIP

ISBN: 0-671-51713-9

Previously published as *Teaching Children Sensitivity*.

We dedicate this book to our three oldest children, Saren, Shawni, and Josh, who, as this book is published, have just finished eighteen months to two years of voluntary, college-interrupting, unpaid humanitarian service and missionary work in Bulgaria, Romania, and England.

We tried to teach them sensitivity as they grew up, but, at some point, they became the teachers and we and their six younger siblings the learners.

Contents

CONTENTS

In 1993 our book *Teaching Your Children Values* hit #1 on the *New York Times* bestseller list. In 1994, Bill Bennett's *Book of Virtues* did the same.

We found ourselves rejoicing in the *interest level* of parents—in their commitment to teaching basic values, despite the opposite direction of much of our popular media.

At the very heart of the values and virtues most parents want for their children is the basic quality of empathy and sensitivity toward other people and toward the beauty and potential of the world and of life itself. Children who learn to *care* and to *feel* vastly expand their potential to be happy as well as their capacity to *give* happiness to those they will love throughout their lives.

Here then is a book about the core virtue of humankind—about the value of sensitivity that can make the lives of our children (and ourselves) full and complete.

Becoming a truly sensitive person involves learning a sequence of skills and awareness levels—all of which takes practice and repetition—none of which can be mastered overnight. The strategy of this book is to work with children on one aspect of sensitivity for a full month—then to move to the next sequential skill for the following month.

In all there are nine abilities—nine separate virtues or aspects of sensitivity, each of which builds on and expands on the previous one and all of which grow together to create the complete quality of a sensitive, caring approach to life. Over the course of several months, you can give this gift to your children . . . and, in the process, you will give it to yourself as well.

—Linda and Richard Eyre
Bear Lake, Idaho   1995

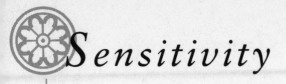

Sensitivity

Psychologists might call it empathy.

Psychiatrists might say extracenteredness.

Christians may recognize it as charity *and quote Scriptures that set it apart as the highest virtue.*

Jews as well as Christians could refer to it as the Golden Rule.

Buddhists, in strikingly similar language, would say seeking for others the happiness you desire for yourself.

In slightly different words, Hindus or Muslims would say the same thing.

Common people of any religion or no religion with common words of any language might just call it service.

And philosophers might name it love of one's neighbor *and might remind us that it is* "the only door out of the dungeon of self"
—G. K. CHESTERTON (ENGLISH AUTHOR, 1874–1936)

We have called it sensitivity. *But we wish the word to mean all of the above. We believe that it can be learned . . . and taught . . . and that it truly can be, both for our children and for ourselves, the door out of the dungeon of self.*

Preface

THIS BOOK HAS BEEN WRITTEN over many years, with input from countless parents. In its earliest editions it was aimed primarily at adolescent-age children based on the premise that of all age groups, teenagers are the most preoccupied with themselves and the least sensitive to others.

But we've come to feel that sensitivity is the key social and emotional need of all children. Small children are often cruel to each other—not a malicious or premeditated cruelty, just an insensitivity—a self-centered lack of awareness of others' feelings.

Empathy is a *learned* ability. Some young children seem to have a special gift for recognizing and caring about how other people feel. Others are more preoccupied with their own needs. So much of what the world teaches them is about themselves, and unless they are taught the importance of sensitivity and the *skills* of observing others, feeling for others, and communicating with others, they will miss many chances to give and receive happiness.

As children grow through the elementary years, they often seem to lose their sweet, caring quality. Once they enter adolescence, their self-awareness becomes almost painful, sometimes leading to self-conscious shyness or withdrawal and sometimes to aggressive rebellion.

As parents we want our children to be happy. We also want them to be responsible and to embrace good values. In working with parents around the globe and with our three previous parenting books (*Teaching Your Children Values, Teaching Your Children Responsibility*, and *Teaching Your Children Joy*), we've become aware that *sensitivity* is the crucial and central element that children must develop if they are to receive the other gifts we try to give them. Most of the traditional values and the sense of responsibility we try to teach our children are based on sensitivity to the needs and rights of others. Happiness, both for ourselves and for our children, is largely the result of a sensitivity to the world and people around us—to beauty and to feelings, to opportunities, and to needs.

Sometimes the best way to define or understand a term is by its opposites. By *sensitivity* we mean the opposite of selfishness, self-centeredness, and self-consciousness—the opposite of the self-focused qualities that George Bernard Shaw said turns men into "selfish, feverish little clods of ailments, complaining that the world will not give us a living."

Sensitivity is a broadening, expanding quality. As the old phrase says, "He who is all wrapped up in himself makes a very small package." The less preoccupation we have with ourselves—with our own needs and comforts—the more we can learn from, appreciate, and enjoy others.

Just as pride, greed, envy, and jealousy turn us inward and make us less aware of everything except what we want, sensitivity turns us outward and makes us less aware of our own little troubles and more aware of the vast world around us—the world of beauty, of opportunity, and of other people.

Sensitivity is the foundation and the reinforcement for so much of what we hope to teach and to give our children. But it is not a simple quality, and it is not easy to teach or to learn. It is a series of skills that need to be developed one at a time and then blended together.

While it may be difficult to develop sensitivity, we've simplified the process by breaking it down like this:

$$U + O + F + C + D = S$$

Understanding + observing + feeling + communicating + doing = sensitivity.

Section 1 is written to help you *understand* the concept of sensitivity as it applies and can be taught to children of various ages.

Section 2 is a collection of workable methods to help children be more *observant*—to see and listen better.

Section 3 is about helping children to be more honest about how they *feel* and more conscious of how others feel.

Section 4 consists of methods to help families and individuals *communicate* better about what they see and feel.

Section 5 is about service, which is the culminating *action* of sensitivity.

Together the sections and their skills add up to sensitivity. Together they can make a difference in how we live and in how we love.

Understanding

A CONCEPTUAL OVERVIEW FOR PARENTS

First is understanding.

An understanding of what sensitivity means in the context of this book.

An understanding of how sensitivity can be learned together by parents and children.

And an understanding about how this book is organized and how you can use it to strengthen your family.

UNDERSTANDING
OBSERVING
FEELING
COMMUNICATING
+ DOING
_____

= SENSITIVITY

A. *Sensitivity: The Ultimate Solution*

We want our children to know what to do ... but it is even more important that they know why. The best "why" is sensitivity—the best reason to do anything is because we care for others as well as for ourselves.

ONE WAY TO DESCRIBE parenting is "one crisis after another."

Perhaps it is so. But it is good to remember that the Chinese character for the word *crisis* is actually a combination of two characters, one meaning "danger," the other "opportunity."

We invite you to view parenting as both a danger and an opportunity, as both a worry and a joy. Let the worry part motivate you to take your parenting task with even greater seriousness. But see the opportunity to help create great human beings and to experience joy. See the opportunity to grow again with your children, to learn to love once again, through them, to "school your feelings" as you learn with them to develop and to exercise empathy and sensitivity.

The sensitivity we speak of is not the self-centered

kind that causes children to get their feelings hurt easily and that causes us as parents to say, "Don't be so sensitive!" Rather it is the extracentered kind of sensitivity that allows children to notice and "sense" the feelings, moods, and needs of others . . . and to respond, serve, and give!

This book is based on a belief that a great many of the problems and concerns of children are based on their self-centeredness. If we can help kids to get their minds *off* themselves and their worries, most of their problems will be solved. If we can get them to get their minds *on* the needs of others, children cease to be part of the problem and become part of the solution. Sensitivity is the name we are giving to this ability to think about others rather than self.

This special sensitivity requires the skills of *observing, feeling, communicating*, and *giving*. The goal of this book is to help parents better learn these skills for themselves and better teach them to their children.

Teaching Sensitivity:
The Greatest Challenge

From the moment we began writing this book, it occurred to us that it would be more difficult than the earlier books in our parenting series (*Teaching Your Children Joy, Teaching Your Children Responsibility*, and *Teaching Your Children Values*). To be truthful, our first thoughts were that teaching joy to preschool children is fun, teaching responsibility to elementary school-age children is difficult, teaching (and living) values is challenging, but teaching kids real sensitivity and empathy toward other people is . . . *impossible*!

Being parents is one of the hardest, most serious jobs around. As we move on from the physically and mentally exhausting job of having little babies, we realize that parenting becomes even more difficult mentally and emotionally as our children become old enough to feel some independence, make decisions, and form relationships.

- How can you get little children who fight and bicker constantly to start thinking about how they are making one another feel?
- How can you help a son who sits in his school classes wondering why everyone hates him realize he should be looking around to see who needs him?
- How can you explain to an adolescent daughter who used to spend all her time helping with little brothers and sisters and now spends most of it in front of the mirror crying because her hair "won't go" that she should be sitting at breakfast with the family and helping with the dishes, regardless of how "horrible" she looks?
- How can you get kids to stop being cruel to a new child in school or to kids who are different in some way? Or how can you help your child understand why other kids are sometimes cruel to him?
- How can you convince a rebellious daughter who thinks you know nothing that you care about her and know some things that can help her?
- How can you teach a son that the most satisfying relationship in the world does not exist between him and his computer?

We are convinced, despite the difficulties, that empathy and sensitivity are qualities we should strive to teach our children, and we believe that there are some good, constructive ways to do this teaching. The first thing to realize, as we will discuss in more detail, is that empathy begins with us! (That's the hardest part.) Often our biggest problem is our inability to put ourselves into our children's shoes. If we could look through their eyes, we would probably see ourselves as parents who are sometimes intolerant and insensitive, anxious and angry, nagging and nasty.

One of the greatest assets we can have, along with empathy, is a sense of humor. The hard job of learning where to draw the line can often be softened with a good laugh—privately as husband and wife, or together as parent and child. Great teaching moments often occur when we can learn to laugh at ourselves.

We have discovered through our own children and through our work with countless numbers of parents and youngsters that it *is* possible to teach sensitivity. The exercises and methods in this book don't work every time with every adolescent. There may be several failures for every success—but that one wonderful success can get parents through the next few crises with a smile and with the insight that sometimes failure teaches as much as success.

Perhaps the most important key in teaching children sensitivity is tenacity—to hang in there and keep trying, never expecting instant results. When you get to the end of your rope, tie a knot and hang on. Winston Churchill said it well: "Never give up . . . never, never, never, never."

What the Book Is About

Teaching Your Children Sensitivity is not meant to be a psychological or analytical book on child behavior, with generalizations about what happens or should happen at each age or phase of development. What it is is a *method* book, with exercises aimed at the objectives of learning and teaching sensitivity. It is an organized, categorized list of techniques to help you increase the sensitivity and the "extracenteredness" of your children . . . and of yourself.

The goal is not so much to make our children into "Good Samaritans" or people who spend their full time doing good turns and serving others. Such a goal with busy, volatile, moody children, as with most adults, would be unrealistic. Most of their service to others will come as they grow up and become contributing adults and parents themselves. The attitudes and skills that go into service and sensitivity, however, can best be developed in our children while they are young. It is the sensitivity-related attitudes and skills that this book is about.

We feel that sensitivity must be learned, one element at a time. We also know that it is difficult for busy parents to concentrate on learning or teaching more than one concept at a time. Thus we have written about one element or one skill that leads to sensitivity in each of nine chapters. We suggest that parents concentrate on one chapter each month, making the book a nine-month program for developing greater sensitivity in themselves and in their children.

Before we get to those one-a-month chapters, however, let's think together about ourselves and our children. The simple fact is that parenting is tough. There aren't any perfect kids. But then again there aren't any perfect parents. There aren't even any perfect solutions for family problems. But there are some things that help! So let's struggle together.

Whom the Book Is For

Although this is a book for all parents, it is meant especially for parents of younger children. There are methods for children as young as three or four and for children as old as fourteen or fifteen. It is a simple fact of life that younger kids are more teachable than sixteen-year-olds. However, having said that, *remember* that *it is never too late*. If you are using this book with older teenagers, you will have to adapt many of the methods—and the best adaptation is when you say to an older teen, "Look, I am going to work on developing more empathy (or giving more service, or some other aspect or skill of the book). Will you work on it *with* me?"

In the method section of each chapter we suggest a range of ideas—some particularly suited to young children, some aimed at eight- to ten-year-olds, and some for adolescents. The methods are always arranged in youngest-to-oldest order.

This book is not written for parents of children with severe problems such as drug addiction, serious criminal activity, or total alienation from family. We leave such problems to experts who are far more qualified to deal with them than we are. Rather this book is written for parents who want a program to *avoid* such severe problems. It is written for parents who want to act rather than re-act, who prefer the positive notion of "parenting by objective" over the negative approach of solving problems when they grow too big to ignore. Our belief is that the best defense is a good offense, that parents who seek to give their children greater capacity for sensitivity will in the process give themselves freedom from many problems that would otherwise arise. We believe that service, empathy, and sensitivity are *preventive medicine*.

But don't get the idea that you can come around to the Eyres' house looking for examples of perfect kids. What you'd find instead are the normal hassles of a house full of children and a couple of amateur parents trying to keep their heads above water. We wrote the book for ourselves along with other struggling parents like ourselves. We wrote it because we want our children to be happy—and we believe that sensitivity and service are keys to that happiness.

One thing that is crucial to your success in using this book is the way in which you *view* your own children. We were recently with a parent who said something like this: "Kids today are such a mess! Not only are they totally self-centered and materialistic, they are downright mean. They're like chickens. Did you know that when you have five or six chickens in the same coop, they find the weakest one among them and they peck him to death? That's the way kids are. They're cruel to each other. They find someone who's a little different or a little shy and they pick on him." This parent's opinion of children's basic nature was obviously not very high. His chicken comparison reminded us of a comparison of kids and crabs that we had seen in a magazine. It told how crabs, when put into shallow buckets in pairs or more than one at a time, could not escape. They were capable of climbing out, but every time one would try, another crab would reach up and pull it back. Children, the article said, are similar; their instinct is to pull others down to their own level.

It is common, even somewhat popular and fashionable, to talk about how impossible today's kids are, how difficult and basically "bad" they are, and to be skeptical about whether anything will "work" with them or about how we could ever really talk to them in a sensible, mature way. Another friend of ours, reading an early manuscript of this book, laughed cynically in several places, saying, "Oh, yes, I can just see me trying *that* with my daughter. She wouldn't have the slightest interest. She wouldn't even give me the time of day, let alone her attention for long enough to try that!"

What we must realize as parents is that we compound our problems (and those of our children) when we insist on making negative assumptions, on thinking of children as chickens or as crabs, on assuming that we can't communicate with them and that their outward surliness is consistent with what is really inside them.

Confucius may have summarized the best way we can view our children with his statue metaphor. He said, "Every piece of marble has a statue in it waiting to be released by a man of sufficient skill to chip away the unwanted parts. You cannot create a statue by smashing the marble with a hammer, and you cannot by force of arms release the spirit or the soul of man." By viewing their child as a beautiful and perfect person somewhat hidden inside a block of selfishness and unwanted tendencies, parents can find the patience and love necessary to chip away the unnecessary parts and set free a sensitive human being who becomes part of the world's solution instead of part of its problem.

This book, then, is for parents who want to take positive, "preventive medicine" approaches—and who want to invite their children to join them in a quest for a more empathic (and thus happier) approach to life.

B. The Problem: "Mirrors"

When life is a window, we see beauty, opportunity, and the needs of others. When life is a mirror, we see only ourselves.

Here are a few stories about ordinary children and the worries of ordinary parents. You won't relate to all of them, but some will be uncomfortably familiar.

1. Patsy: *respect and authority.* Patsy, age nine, has recently become a know-it-all. Suddenly no one, particularly her parents, can tell her anything. In fact simultaneously with her becoming a know-it-all, her parents have become know-nothings. She questions everything, especially their authority over her. She is critical of her family, her friends, how people dress, and just about everything but herself. She has become obnoxiously outspoken about everything and is extremely hard to be around.

2. Jeremy: *motivation and the question, "Why?"* Jeremy, age eight, is lazy. He's a bright enough boy; his IQ tests have always confirmed that. But he is also, according to the school counselor, a "severe underachiever." His best grades are mediocre. His favorite activity is sitting in front of the TV. His parents have tried everything, from bribery to punishment and penalties of all kinds. Jeremy's favorite response, to everything from "Get your room straightened up" to "You can't succeed without good grades," is "Why?"

3. *Justin: propriety.* It sounds funny to say it about a four-year-old, but Justin has no sense of propriety. His loud and demanding nature are doubly difficult to deal with when he acts out in *public* by screaming or yelling for what he needs. His mother has tried everything to get him to *notice* other people around him and to be aware that his behavior is bothering them, but to no avail.

4. *Allison: shyness and sociability.* Allison, age eleven, is usually talkative, even boisterous at home. She is a bright, attractive girl and has never been without opinions or hesitant to express them. Her parents have always been confused when teachers told them that Allison was painfully shy at school. Occasionally in moments of frustration Allison expresses her pain: "No one likes me." "Everyone ignores me." "I'm so sick of sitting all by myself in the lunchroom." "Sometimes I just sit alone in the hall trying to look busy and hoping people don't notice that I'm always by myself." "Why doesn't somebody pay attention to me?"

5. *Steve and Susan: constant fighting.* Steve and Susan, ages eight and six, fight with each other constantly. They fight over everything, from who knows the most about baseball to who gets to sit in the front seat. Neither one will ever give in or admit that the other could be right.

6. *Larry: drugs and independence.* Larry, age thirteen,

has a drug problem. It's not an addiction problem so much as an experimentation problem. It's hard for him to resist trying things, particularly when his friends push him. His parents don't know much about it. They suspect that he's "on" something or other, but there's not much communication between them and Larry. The only adult Larry talks to is his uncle Bill, who takes Larry hunting and fishing and who respects his confidence. In their last discussion Larry said, "Life is boring. The only thing that makes it interesting is trying new things. The guys I hang around with are a lot more exciting than the other kids. We're finding out things for ourselves, without our parents. They wouldn't want to know about this anyway."

7. *Barret: language.* Barret is eight and lives in a nice suburban area, but his language is filthy. His mother overhears him talking with his friends and using the "F-word" frequently.

8. *Derrick: peer pressure and sex.* Derrick is as aware of peer approval as any normal fourteen-year-old boy. He's put on some inches and pounds lately and improved as a ballplayer, which has allowed him to crack the "in-crowd" at school. His new friends brag about their exploits with girls; Derrick is never sure how much of it is just talk and how much they have really done. He wants to have something to talk about, too, and although he certainly doesn't want to get into trouble, he *is* influenced by his peers, who tell him that "there's no problem as long as you use a condom."

9. *Diedra: intolerance and cruelty toward other children.* Diedra, age seven, seems to be a model child in many ways. She is intelligent, friendly, well liked, a leader in most everything. She is the apple of everyone's eye, particularly her parents' and teachers'. But Diedra isn't very

sensitive to other people's needs. She assumes that everyone else is as happy as she. It hasn't occurred to her that her own security and self-esteem could be *shared* or given as a gift to other children who need it. While friendly and courteous to adults and to her friends, she is openly critical and sometimes abusive of children who are a little different, a little shy, a little "out of place." This criticism sometimes takes the form of ridicule and outright cruelty.

10. Conrad: *maturity and moodiness.* Even though he is nearly fifteen, Conrad is very immature. He relies on his parents as much as or more than his eleven-year-old brother does. He gets sick rather often and seems to enjoy staying home in bed, where his mother can wait on him. He cries often and tends to sulk when he doesn't get his way. He likes books and lately spends most of his time in his bedroom alone reading.

11. Sheridon: *teasing and name-calling.* Sheridon, age five, has recently perfected the art of teasing her three-year-old brother. She takes things from him, pulls his hair, calls him names, and the more he screams, the more she does it.

12 Laura: *self-esteem and the right friends.* Laura, age twelve, has started to talk a lot lately about "being depressed." And she does more than talk about it! She is negative about everything. She feels that everyone is against her and talks a lot about how stupid she is. She expects the worst and she gets it. She peps up a little when she is with her friends. But they are, in her parents' eyes, mostly "the wrong type." Her mother has urged her to make friends with more of the kids in her own neighborhood, to which Laura makes a horrible face and replies, "Mom, that depresses me."

13. Norman: *hyperactivity and attention span.* Norman's mom describes him as "a nine-year-old hyperactive social butterfly who never lights." From the time he was a small boy, Norm has loved people. He would bring a different friend home from school every afternoon if allowed. *But he can't stay with anything.* His attention span is about five seconds long. He's been taking piano lessons for nearly three years and has made very little progress because he can't discipline himself to practice. Grades, sports, and other interests suffer for the same lack of discipline.

14. Karen: lack of respect for property. Karen simply has no respect for other people's property. Her parents cannot seem to get her to put anything away, and she seems to lose or ruin something every day.

15. Lisa: honesty and rationalization. When Lisa was younger, her parents were sometimes amused by the imaginative excuses she came up with. Her untruths were so creative that it was hard for them to get mad at her. But Lisa is ten now, and her "little lies" have ceased to be amusing. Her account of things is always whatever is most convenient or advantageous for her, whether it is true or not. And with this dishonesty has come a remarkable ability to rationalize. Both abilities combined recently in a case or two of shoplifting. She hasn't told her parents of course and will deny it if she is ever asked. And if she is ever caught, she will explain that the store deserved it since their prices are too high.

16. Billy: bullying. Billy is six, and he's a bully. He's a little bigger than most of the kids in his class and he's found that he can get attention (and get his way) by shoving or hitting other children. When his mother tries to correct him, he hits her.

17. Glen: tidiness and responsibility. Glen, who is

twelve, has not "grown out of it." His messy room and general untidiness are a problem of long duration, but one his parents have tolerated in the hope that he would mature. Instead it has become worse. He can never find anything. His own room is literally hard to get into or out of. And he leaves what his mother calls a trail of disaster in every room he passes through.

18. Jill: fad consciousness and inconsideration toward family. The highlight of eleven-year-old Jill's week is her shopping trip to the mall on Saturdays. She's only satisfied with the right brand name or the thing everyone else is wearing no matter how expensive it is. She screams when she finds her sister wearing the only shoes that go with the outfit she spent hours last night picking out, and stubbornly refuses to go to school until she gets them back. And she cannot understand how her mother could have forgotten to wash her gym clothes on Friday.

❋ ❋ ❋

What is similar about the behavior of the children in these vignettes? "Very little," we might answer. Some are rowdy and rebellious, the opposite of those who are painfully shy and withdrawn. Some are fad conscious and aggressive, whereas others are unaware and lazy.

But in fact all of these kids are more similar to each other than their behavior indicates. Despite the wide variations in how it manifests itself, what they all have in common is the highly typical childhood tendency toward self-centeredness and self-preoccupation.

Once we are able to separate the symptoms from the cause, we can begin to consider the remedy.

Symptoms Versus Causes

In the case of most diseases the symptoms are the manifestations of the cause, and the cause is due to the presence of something, namely a virus or bacteria.

In the case of children the symptoms are the kinds of behavior illustrated in the preceding short stories and the cause is due to the *absence* of something.

Therefore we can ask ourselves whether there is something that could prevent or reduce such varied symptoms as shyness, rebellion, obnoxiousness, laziness, dishonesty, and selfishness.

We feel that sensitivity is the "preventative medicine" for children because:

- Sensitivity is a way of *thinking*: a form of thought that includes observing and feeling, communicating and giving.
- When we change the way in which someone thinks, we change the way he or she acts.
- When approached in the right way, no age group is more capable of changing how they think than children.

Mirrors

A great many of the problems children face and most of the unhappiness they experience results from their natural tendency to "look into mirrors." Most people, and particularly children, tend to see situations, people, and circumstances in terms of how those things will affect *them*. And when these mirrors become dominant and extreme, they *cause* rebellion, depression, selfishness, disrespect, bizarre behavior, self-consciousness, and a host of other symptoms.

Too often when children look at another person, what they see is the mirror of their own feelings and fears. ("He's getting a lot of attention; maybe I should do what he's doing!" "What can he do for me?" "How will my reputation be affected by associating with her?" "Will it cost me anything to be nice to her?")

When people with "mirror problems" look at a situation or an event, what they see is what they can gain or lose by it. They prove the cliche that says, "Someone who is all wrapped up in himself makes a very small package." And perhaps a rather erratic and unhappy package at that!

Mirrors have no depth. We see only the surface of ourselves when we look into them. One who stares into mirrors continually is only fleetingly happy, and this happiness is never stable or predictable because every change of light, perspective, or circumstance threatens the image and changes the feeling.

Our goal should be to remove some of our children's mirrors.

But wait a moment, you say. If we are going to accuse our children of looking into mirrors, we had better examine ourselves first. Everyone probably thinks of himself or herself an inordinate amount of time, and if we are going to teach our children to be less self-centered, we had better teach ourselves the same lesson first.

Exactly!

As you read on, you will see that this principle is the order of our book: First teach a particular aspect of sensitivity to yourself, then teach it to your children.

C. *The Prescription:* "*Windows*"

SOME SOLUTIONS FOR ORDINARY PROBLEMS

The right kind of sensitivity gives those who have it both personal confidence and personal humility, along with empathy for others. These are tools that fix any break, prescriptions that cure any ill.

Mirrors and Windows

Some older civic and church buildings still have "cry rooms" just off the chapel or meeting area where parents can retreat to with extra-noisy babies. Many of these cry rooms feature a pane of one-way glass, which is a mirror to those sitting in the meeting room and a window to those sitting in the cry room looking out.

Metaphorically all of us are surrounded by such one-way glass. Turned one way, the glass is a mirror, causing us to view all of life as a self-centered reflection of ourselves. But we each have the power to reverse the glass, to turn mirrors into windows. Doing so is an important step in attaining sensitivity. For these windows of sensitivity are the solution to virtually every childhood and family difficulty.

Extracentered Sensitivity:
What It Is and How It Works

Both self-centeredness and extracenteredness tend to be self-perpetuating and self-magnifying. An extracentered person radiates the kind of awareness and interest *in* others that makes him or her more interesting *to* others. Interest and friendliness from others then increases a person's awareness of others and magnifies his or her extracenteredness still farther. On the other hand, self-centered persons give off signals of unawareness and disinterest in others that wall them off and turn their awareness even farther inward toward themselves.

Someone who learns the skills (observing, feeling, communicating, giving) of sensitivity steadily becomes less aware of self and more aware of others and thus grows progressively more extracentered.

This process can be diagrammed as a triangle:

As we work with our children to develop in them a greater awareness of others, we "stretch" the triangle, improving their ability to get their minds off themselves and lengthening the base of extracenteredness that we are calling sensitivity.

As one's extracenteredness increases, something of a personal miracle happens. A person becomes steadily more aware of the nature of others and of their needs, concerns, and situations—and more aware of the differences between himself and them. As this happens, a person sees himself more accurately while thinking about

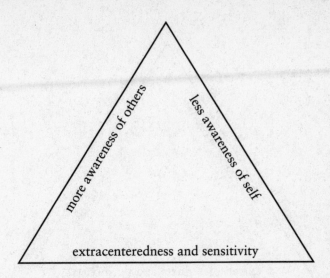

himself less. The result is a greater appreciation of personal uniqueness and less inclination to want to be just like everyone else. A person becomes less interested in following the crowd and more interested in discovering his own best self. He also becomes more naturally inclined toward *service* and mutually helpful *involvement* with other people.

We can add to our triangle:

With this model in mind let's return to our "ordinary problems" and see how much an increased dose of extracenteredness or sensitivity might help in each case.

Short Stories Revisited
As a person develops greater extracentered sensitivity and gives more service, he or she becomes:

1. More aware of others
2. Less aware of self

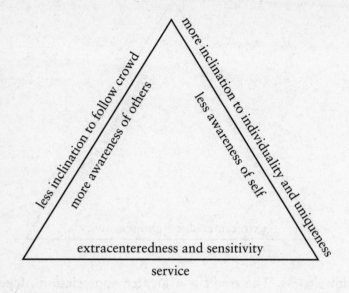

3. Less inclined to follow the crowd and less dependent on the approval of peers

4. More inclined to perceive and appreciate his or her own uniqueness and to develop self-confidence because of it

Refer back to the earlier vignettes and consider which of the four aspects of sensitivity noted above are needed by each child.

1. More awareness of others. Regarding know-it-all Patsy (#1, in Chapter B), cruel Diedra (#9), dishonest Lisa (#15), demanding Justin (#3), disrespectful Karen (#14), and sloppy Glen (#17), each of their symptoms is a direct outgrowth of their lack of awareness of others and their insensitivity to the needs of others.

2. *Less awareness of self.* In the cases of shy, self-conscious Allison (#4), moody, immature Conrad (#10), hyperactive Norman (#13), fighting siblings Steve and Susan (#5), and fad-conscious Jill (#18), a less intense and constant awareness of self is the prescription.

3. *Less dependency on the approval of peers.* What peer-pressured Derrick (#8), drug-experimenting Larry (#6), foul-mouthed Barret (#7), and depressed Laura (#12) need is less dependency on peer approval, less inclination to follow the crowd.

4. *Greater awareness of own uniqueness and self-confidence.* Besides an escape from peer approval, Laura (#12) needs more self-esteem and a stronger appreciation of her own uniqueness. Shy Allison (#4), unmotivated Jeremy (#2), immature Conrad (#10), flighty Norman (#13), bully Billy (#16), and teasing Sheridon (#11) could also clear up their problems with the extra self-confidence that increased sensitivity would give them.

Look back at our second triangle model again. Can increased extracenteredness, sensitivity, and service really increase a person's awareness of others and the accuracy with which that person sees his or her own uniqueness? Can this added sensitivity at the same time improve self-image and individuality and decrease self-consciousness and the need for peer approval?

The answer is yes on both counts. The real solution to the problem of each child in each of the stories lies in sensitivity. Added sensitivity could help turn their mirrors into windows, removing the self-centeredness that produces shyness in some, laziness and immaturity in others, and rudeness and rebellion in still others.

Again, children are not the only ones who need to turn mirrors into windows. Some of the problems discussed in the stories resulted from a lack of sensitivity not in the children but in their parents.

Self-oriented, mirror-gazing parents may become annoyed by minor amounts of normal childhood and adolescent nonconformity because of its impact on their own image or reputation. Or they may become personally hurt or offended by the new independence and strong opinions of a teenager, instead of understanding that such breaking away is a normal and healthy part of growing up.

Parents who had acquired the qualities of extracenteredness and sensitivity would be able to understand the need for independence being expressed in various ways by the children in these stories. They would think more of the evolving needs of their children and less of their own inconvenience or embarrassment. And as they tried to teach their children the principles of sensitivity, their own empathy would allow them to look for the unique and real characters of their children rather than trying to make them over into their own preconceptions of what they should be.

Sensitivity, then, as it is developed by parents and taught to children, becomes something of a panacea. It becomes a solution for some problems, an eliminator of others, and a preventative for still others.

But this type of empathetic sensitivity, involving the capacities of understanding, seeing, feeling, communicating, and giving, is not easy to learn or to teach. It is these hard-to-learn capacities at which this book takes aim, suggesting methods, techniques, and ideas through which they can be both given and gained.

How to Read and Implement This Book

The capacities, abilities, or skills that go into sensitivity are like the facets of a well-cut stone. Each supports and enhances the others and contributes to the beauty of the whole.

From here on, the book is organized into *months*. The idea is to take one aspect or characteristic of sensitivity and work or focus on it for an entire month. Each month contains methods, ideas, and techniques on how to develop one particular element of sensitivity and how to teach it to your children. Some of the methods outlined for each month will appeal to you and will work with your children. Others will not. Pick out the ones that ring true for you and read past the ones that don't. Use a flexible approach: Look at all the ideas, try on those you like, and keep the ones that fit and *feel* the best. Remember that within each chapter or month the methods are arranged with those that apply to younger children coming first.

Many of the suggestions require some individual time with children. Try to find ways to spend time together despite your busy world. Form habits of a brief talk at bedtime or first thing in the morning or right after dinner, or take a child with you in the car as you run an errand.

As you get into the nine-month program that follows, you will discover that each month suggests a "family focal point"—a method to make ongoing and habitual in your family, perhaps done on Sundays. This springs from our feeling that the first day of the week should be a day of renewal as well as rest. We also feel that Sunday is an especially appropriate time to work together on aspects of sensitivity. Therefore activities such as Sunday planning sessions, family discussions, and even a weekly "awards ceremony" are recommended for Sundays as ongoing patterns for steadily developing various facets of sensitivity.

If parents plan well, they can set aside some time on Sunday (it may have to be early in the morning or later in the evening or built around Sunday dinner) to work with children on the skills this book teaches. Sundays thus become a time of progress as well as a checkpoint where we try to measure the improvements we are making as students of sensitivity.

You will also notice that some methods are used in more than one month. For example certain writing techniques (especially journal writing and poetry), perception games, awards, and even the use of "ancestor experiences" are introduced in more than one chapter. Certain concepts and words, such as *mental effort* and *serendipity*, are also repeated. This repetition is intentional, because the methods work in more than one way and the concepts apply to more than one skill. Most importantly they are repeated because they are so relevant to the encouragement of true sensitivity that they benefit us more each time we use them.

Our challenge to you is to implement the rest of the book one month at a time, to use the methods and suggestions that you like and add your own ideas to them, and to invest nine months in the pursuit, discovery, and teaching of sensitivity.

The Format

Although this book follows an "equation" and is designed to be absorbed and implemented one month at a time, you may (and we hope you will) read through the book first, then return to "Month 1" and spend a full thirty days on it with your family, then a second month on "Month 2," and so on. We believe that a key to effective parenting (and to effective living, for that matter) is to concentrate on one thing at a time. In one month behavior patterns can be established as good habits that will continue after the teaching emphasis has shifted to the next month.

Each of the nine months, although dealing with a different aspect of sensitivity, has the same format and the same five subheadings:

1. *Illustrations and stories* (to define what we are dealing with).
2. *Approaches for parents* (to improve our own grasp of the trait or aspect of charity being discussed—to teach it to ourselves).
3. *Exercises to teach children* (to help them *absorb* the quality). This section will always begin with a family discussion and a little prequiz to measure how much children know about the month's subject. It will always end with a postquiz to measure what they (and you) have learned during the month. (Older children can take them in writing, younger ones can do them verbally in discussion with you.) These discussions and tests are suggested for the first Sunday of the month. During them you will finish your concentration on the past month's subject and start your concentration on the aspect of sensitivity to be dealt with

in the month ahead. After the pretest the methods and teaching exercises are listed in youngest-to-oldest order, with brief descriptions of what each is intended to accomplish.

4. *Family focal point* (a suggestion for one permanent family practice or procedure in order to retain that particular quality of sensitivity in your family's behavior even as your focus shifts to another chapter and another facet of sensitivity).

5. *Summary*

Getting Started: The Family Meeting

A family meeting or "first Sunday discussion," consisting simply of getting everyone together for a few minutes, is the opening method for each of the following nine months. (Sunday is the most "accessible" day for most families, but meet on whatever day and time is convenient—*early* in the week.) Most of the family-meeting ideas are aimed at children of at least elementary school age.

The meeting can be held regardless of the size of your family. If you have only one or two children, you have the advantage of being able to turn this meeting into a personal chat. If your family is larger, you have the advantage of more interaction and mutual stimulation.

It would be nice to tell you that the first time you ring the bell for a family meeting, your children will run right to you and wait for instructions. But this probably won't be the case. A little preparation is called for, as well as a little patience. Announce a few days prior to the meeting that a special family meeting will be held on Sunday. Build up excitement for it by reminding the children of it several times. When the appointed time arrives, plan on running into some difficulties, such as: (a) friends in the house, whom you will have to send home, or (b) excuses about not coming to the meeting because of a ball game, a TV show, or a prior commitment with friends. (If none of these excuses work, they will try something even more compelling, such as "I've got hours and hours of homework that I've just *got* to get started on.")

Help to overcome these difficulties by telling the children that what you have in mind will make a difference in the family that will contribute to everyone's well-being— much more than the TV show, the activity with their friends, or even their homework.

The first meeting will probably be the hardest, but after that—especially if you can establish a specific time and place on the first Sunday of each month—the family meeting will happen with much less resistance.

You can set the tone of the first meeting by making it clear to your children that *you* are going to be working on becoming more sensitive and that you are inviting them to join you *because* you feel that they are old enough and capable enough to do so.

When we held this first Sunday meeting in our family, we began by putting the very young children to bed a little early and announcing that the others could stay up with us for something special we had planned. We sat around the dining room table together and ate ice cream and then we eased into a discussion based on four questions:

1. *What is sensitivity?* Being more aware of others, less aware of self; noticing others, feeling empathy

with them, communicating these feelings well; seeking to give what others need.

2. *What are the connections between sensitivity and happiness?* Practicing sensitivity makes others happy as well as ourselves; it takes our minds off of ourselves; it gives us warm feelings; it makes the world a better place.

3. *What are the differences between a person who looks "into mirrors" and one who looks "through windows"?* The first is more selfish; more worried about clothes, looks, popularity, and such; and is usually more stressed and unhappy; the second is kinder, notices more, is nicer to be around.

4. *What are the abilities or skills that would help someone to exercise more sensitivity and to look "through more windows"?* Abilities to see and observe, to listen, to feel, to communicate, and to think of ways to help others, along with an understanding of what sensitivity is.

On a sheet of paper we wrote the equation:

UNDERSTANDING + OBSERVING + FEELING +
COMMUNICATION + DOING = SENSITIVITY

Then we essentially said, "We (your parents) have decided to spend the next few months working on our own sensitivity. We want to work on one part of this equation each month. We'd like to invite you to do this with us. Each first Sunday we'll have a discussion like this about the part of sensitivity that we'll be working on during the coming month."

The children seemed to understand most of what was

said. They supplied some of the answers and they could think of examples or illustrations for some of the answers we gave. And they were willing if not anxious to meet again and get started on the first month (particularly if ice cream would again be served).

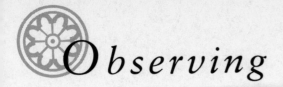

Observing

We *can't appreciate or sympathize until we learn to* see.

We *can't empathize or understand until we learn to* listen.

We *can't forget ourselves until we learn to* notice others.

The *first step toward sensitivity is called* observing.

UNDERSTANDING
OBSERVING
FEELING
COMMUNICATING
+ DOING
_____

= SENSITIVITY

Seeing

"If I had influence with the good fairy who is supposed to preside over the christening of all children, I should ask that her gift to each child be a sense of wonder so indestructible that it would last throughout life, an unfailing antidote against boredom . . . disenchantment . . . preoccupation with things that are artificial."

RACHEL CARSON

"Only that day dawns to which we are awake."

HENRY DAVID THOREAU

Sensitivity is both a feeling and a skill, and the development of the skill deepens the feeling.

Illustrations and Stories

Roman emperor Marcus Aurelius (AD 121–80) said, "We ought to do good to others as simply and as naturally as a horse runs, or a bee makes honey, or a vine bears grapes season after season without thinking of the grapes it has borne."

Unfortunately what we ought to do is not what we

usually *do* do. It is possible to have service and sensitivity come naturally and easily to us, but not without a long process of conditioning.

As we master the skills of seeing, of listening, of sensitivity and empathy, we develop the *habits* of service. Then and only then will we do good to others as naturally as a horse runs.

The skills and habits that lead us to acts of service and the feelings that constitute love and sensitivity are like chicken and egg. One who deeply feels the love of parents and others he or she is close to will find it natural to care, to listen, to empathize, and to serve. On the other hand one who consciously and conscientiously learns these observing, listening, and empathizing skills and develops habits of service will find that they lead him or her to a deeper and more purposeful love of others.

We learn to love by loving. It is the *doing* that develops the *feeling*. Saint Francis of Sales said it better than we can: "You learn to speak by speaking, to study by studying, to run by running, to work by working; and just so you learn to love . . . by loving. Begin as a mere apprentice and the very power of love will lead you on to become a master of the art."

So how do we apprentice at the art of loving? Well, we first have to think more about other people and about their needs—and less about ourselves.

How do we think more about others?

We strive to *notice* more, to learn to observe others with mind as well as with eyes, with heart as well as with brain.

So are we saying that *seeing* is the first skill in the formula for sensitivity?

Yes!

Most people have had the experience of watching a movie that was filmed in a place with which they were familiar. Yet they notice things in the movie that they did not see when they were there in person.

Oftentimes in fact movies seem more graphic to us than real life. We observe beauty, colors, characteristics about people, subtle messages in facial expressions, and so on. Part of our increased awareness may be due to the skill of the cinematographer and the actors, but part of it is due to the very interesting fact that we see more when we are concentrating on seeing and when we're not able to be seen by those we're watching. Since we are not aware of or concerned with what others are seeing in us, we can focus all of our attention on them—thus we notice more and understand more. We only have a certain amount of awareness. If a portion of it is focused on ourselves, there is less left to observe others.

There are people who have learned to become "transparent," to become invisible enough to themselves that they can see *through* themselves and out at others, using all of their attention and awareness to do so. For them life is somewhat like a movie, not in the sense that they are not involved and present but in the sense that they are able to see and observe fully without the distraction of self-consciousness.

We have a friend who is a doctor in a small Idaho town. He practices every kind of medicine on every kind of patient. He told us once that he occasionally runs into someone who has become such a proficient observer that he can detach himself and watch everything, even himself. Such patients, says the doctor, can rise above not only their emotions and self-consciousness but even above their pain. They *observe* their pain. It is, in a way, *interesting* to them. They wonder if the pain will increase, how much it will increase, how they will react if it does increase. It is as though they are watching a movie of themselves.

We once knew a basketball coach who talked in much the same way about some of his best players from over the years. In pressure situations, instead of "clutching"—becoming stressed and tense with self-awareness and with the possibilities of being a hero or a failure—they became interested in how they would respond, what they might do, whether they had what it takes to make the right play. They watched everything, even themselves, with the interested, entertained, insightful eye of the trained observer.

It is ironic how we say, "Don't just be a spectator, an observer of life. Get involved." In reality, those who have learned to truly observe are the very ones who do become meaningfully and effectively involved.

There is a best-selling tennis book called *Inner Tennis*, which applies many of the techniques of Zen and of meditation to the game. The book claims that if we can learn to truly watch what is happening, including what we are doing, we will know exactly what to change, what to do, where to improve. In other words, most tennis players have already seen enough good tennis to know how to hit shots properly. Their body, their inner self, knows how, but their mind is telling them things like "pull your racket back, don't over hit, keep your knees bent, watch the ball" so insistently that they become stressed, awkward, and self-conscious.

Just learn to watch, to observe, the book says. When you *see* what you are doing, you will make your own adjustments.

Life is the same. When we are always judging ourselves, comparing ourselves with others, wondering what so-and-so thinks of us, concerned about how we look, we become unable to observe, unable to see what is happening around us; unable to notice what others are doing, thinking, needing; and even unable to see ourselves accurately and objectively.

A law of mathematics is "If you can clearly and accurately see and define the problem, you can solve it."

A law of baseball is "If you can see the ball clearly as well as the spin that's on it, you can hit it."

A law of life is "If you can see people clearly, you can love them."

Approaches for Parents

The approaches that follow will enhance your seeing capacity and will increase your motivation as well as your ability to teach this first facet of sensitivity.

We get so wrapped up in the mundane busywork of life that we often forget to be sensitive ourselves. I was standing at the kitchen sink not long ago hurrying to get dinner, directing homework activities, and talking on the phone at the same time. As always, our four-year-old picks these times to need something. He kept pulling on my skirt and pounding on my leg, saying, "Mommy, look at this, look at this, look at this." After about the tenth time he had repeated it, I glanced down, expecting to see a picture he'd drawn or a feather he'd found, but instead he pointed to a little bruise on his arm.

I kept talking, and he kept pounding. Finally I excused myself from the caller, held my hand over the receiver, and said in exasperation, "Eli, I see your bruise, but I don't know what you want me to do about it. A Band-Aid won't help. What do you want me to do?" In his innocent little way he said, "Well, Mom, you could say, 'Oh dear!' " All he needed was for me to acknowledge that he was hurt and to sympathize a little.

As we try to teach our children to see more and to observe with greater sympathy and awareness, we must also be anxious to do better ourselves, to *develop* our own awareness. Following are some suggestions for doing so:

1. Write poetry. This may seem, at first glance, like a rather strange suggestion, particularly to put at the top of a list, but the writing of poetry, even the attempt to write poetry, is one of the most dramatically effective ways we know to sharpen awareness and observation skills.

Good poets are essentially people who look at the same things we do but see more. They see interrelationships between things; they intensely see form and color; they see (or at least the good ones do) the inner, unexpressed feelings of people around them. We are convinced that many of these "watchers" have not learned to be poets because they can observe, rather they have learned to observe because they are poets.

Attempts to capture beliefs or beauty, sentiments or situations, in a small number of carefully chosen words are efforts at poetry, and they cause one to *look* hard and really to *see*.

We are not suggesting that parents must write the kind of poetry Emily Dickinson spoke of: "If I read a book and it makes my whole body so cold no fire can warm me, I know that is poetry. If I feel physically as if the top of my head were taken off, I know that is poetry. These are the only ways I know it. Is there any other way?" No, the poetry we amateurs write doesn't have to take anyone's head off, and it doesn't even have to be shown to anyone! It can be private. The benefit is in the process of writing (and observing).

Try an experiment. Start modestly. Decide to attempt two small poems a week for the next month, about a sunset, about a child, about anything. Just the commitment to try will cause you to start noticing more and to start thinking about what you observe!

2. *Keep a journal.* An alternative to poetry (or better yet, a companion to it) is journal writing, particularly if efforts are made to describe your experiences and ideas. Description is the fruit of our observations. We can describe only what we have observed. Our journals, in addition to being a living record of our lives and times, can be the evidence of our observations and can actually cause us to notice more in our children and in other associations than we would otherwise.

3. *Keep "blank books."* Still another writing method, and the one we like best, is the "blank book." We decided to get some hard-bound books of good manuscript paper, one for each child, and to write our observations of that child periodically, every few months, in the form of an ongoing letter to the child. When the children get married, one wedding present will be their book containing their parents' lifelong observations and feelings about them.

Our motive for starting the blank books, besides creating something nice for our children, was to encourage ourselves to think very thoroughly about each of them as they were growing up. These books have caused us to observe our children better and to notice them more. Often what we see and what we write in describing what we see becomes a process by which we discover and solve problems—before they get too big.

4. See the humor in life. Next to poets, comedians may be the best observers. One needs to notice and closely observe things before one can be funny about them. Cultivating a sharper sense of humor and learning to observe more closely are two parts of another chicken-egg situation. Each leads to the other.

Perhaps the most valuable kind of humor to develop is the kind that allows us to laugh at ourselves, to avoid the heavy, overseriousness that usually indicates we are thinking (and worrying) too much about ourselves.

Take the time to sit around and do nothing with your children once in a while. Change your perspective a little and get on their level. Just talk. Joke with them, laugh with them. Fit in with them. Relax and find some easy, natural humor in day-to-day situations.

5. Watch children. The simplest method for observing our children is the best one. It is simply to set aside an hour to do nothing but watch. Follow them around but stay back so that you are not a participant or an interference but a nonthreatening observer. And *watch, watch*! What interests the child, how does she approach different situations, how does he react to others? Think about what you see. Make notes.

6. Your own methods. Occasionally as you read through the suggested approaches for parents, other ideas will occur to you, other methods or exercises by which you could further practice or develop your own ability in the skill we are aiming at in a particular month. Use the space provided to write down those ideas. Make your ideas a part of your copy of this book. Begin (this month) by thinking about other ways to increase your awareness or "seeing" ability.

Exercises to Teach Children

1. *First-Sunday discussion.* This activity is designed to establish, within the minds of all family members, the goals of seeing and observing more closely during the coming month. (Note: The first method mentioned in each chapter is a "first-Sunday discussion." The first Sunday of the month becomes the transitional time, when you shift your attention from one aspect of sensitivity to another).

Begin by telling the children that during the coming month you want to concentrate on a skill that will help you to "look through windows" and become aware of others. It is the skill of observing. Explain that observing means looking closely, *really* seeing. Discuss why powers of observation are so important and make a list of what you come up with. For example, observing

- Adds enjoyment to life
- Helps us live more in the present
- Permits us to recognize opportunities
- Prevents us from missing things
- Helps us notice the needs of others
- Is the best method of education
- Gives us more to talk about
- Makes every day more interesting

Adapt the discussion to the ages of your children. Point out that observing is *fun*, and that it is fun to have a goal together as a family (the goal of improving powers of observation). Mention that the goal can be reached only if we help each other. Several people can observe more than one person alone, and you can *remind* each other to observe.

In our family this was our second "sensitivity meeting." (That was our name for it; the kids called it the second "ice-cream meeting.")

The older children were impressed with the mirror-and-window analogy. They could see that people who looked through windows would be happier (and would make others happier) than people who looked into mirrors.

We told them about some of the "seeing games" we would play during the month ahead (see the following exercises), and our competitive eleven-year-old got excited about beating us in some of the contests.

If you have children age eight or older, continue the discussion along the following lines:

• Read the Rachael Carson quote from the first page of this chapter and ask what it means.

2. Prequiz. Say, "To help us measure how much we each learn about observing this month, we're going to take a short quiz today on how much we notice and how much we try to describe what we see. At the end of the month we'll take the quiz again to see how much we've improved."

Have each family member who is old enough to write put his or her name on a piece of paper and draw a line down the center. Include yourself. Explain that your answers today will go on the left side of the page and that the right side will be used when you retake the test at the end of the month. Then answer the following:

• How many times during the past month have you:

Written a poem

Described something or written an observation in your journal

• Write the most detailed description you can of:

The room you sleep in

Your school room, homeroom, or office

Your best friend

The most interesting nose you saw last month

Kids may write very little on this first test since they haven't observed much. Tell them not to worry—*it's not really a test.* It's just something to come back to at the end of the month to see how much we've learned.

3. Nature walks. These will enable your family to practice observation skills and will help you to create peaceful teaching moments. The best place to practice observing is the place where there is most to observe. Nature is a great teacher. There are things to be learned from everything we see, and metaphors for life are everywhere we look.

Russian novelist Fyodor Dostoyevsky said:

> "Love all of God's creations, both the whole and every grain of sand. Love every leaf, every ray of light. Love the animals, love the plants, love each separate thing. If thou love each thing, thou will perceive the mystery of God in all; and when once thou perceive this, thou will thenceforward grow every day to a fuller understanding of it; until thou come at last to love the whole world with a love that will then be all embracing and universal."

Dostoyevsky was essentially describing sensitivity, and he claimed that observing and loving nature is the gateway to it.

American botanist George Washington Carver said, "I love to think of nature as an unlimited broadcasting station, through which God speaks to us every hour, if we will only listen."

You don't necessarily have to go to a national park or a vast forest or climb a high mountain to experience and observe nature. But you do have to be somewhat alone with a child and to have a focused feeling of calmness and solitude. A park, a creekside, a stand of trees, a garden, even a backyard or a sunset: we don't have to look very hard to find nature. We just have to look hard to really *see* it.

Take a walk and see what you can observe together. Make it a game if you wish—who can point out what to the other. Try to notice things you have never seen before. Think and talk about why they are the way they are. Look for comparisons to make between what you see and some aspect of your life.

For example, we were walking (two daughters and their dad) along a small, narrow trail in a summer canyon. The girls were picking flowers, seeing who could find the most different kinds. We were comparing them, noticing their petal structure, trying to decide where each kind would grow, observing how strikingly different each flower type was from every other variety. We came to some large dandelion-type flowers that had gone to seed and started blowing the tiny parachutes into the blue sky and watching them float on the breeze. The six-year-old picked a large, perfectly round one and held it up to the sun so that the nob in the center of the radiating parachute seeds covered the sun in her eye. She showed us how the sunlight dazzled the white seeds, turning the flower into a shimmering round crystal. The eight-year-old said she thought each dandelion had over a hundred seeds and that each one was just slightly different from all the rest. That led us into a little discussion of individuality and of how every person is completely unique.

4. Observing-noses game. This is an enjoyable way to practice observation skills and to impress children with how much variety and uniqueness there is in the world. Pick a certain day and have everyone in the family observe noses. Tell the children that at supper that night you will discuss the most interesting noses each person saw that day. Have them look for long noses, hook noses, "ski jump" noses, pug noses, and so on. Ask them to remember the noses they find interesting so that they can describe them. Be careful with this method—and teach a little discretion. We have one child who enjoyed the game so much that she still points out (to everyone within earshot) every interesting nose that she sees.

5. *Optical illusions.* This exercise is intended to increase interest in observation and to teach children that people can be fooled by quick, careless observation. Any library can be the source of books with interesting optical illusions (such as the old woman–young woman picture, in which some see one face and others see another; or pictures where two lines of equal length appear unequal). Such books can promote lively interest and discussion and can open opportunities to talk about observing and looking carefully at things. The popular "magic eye" books also illustrate that there is more than one way to look at things.

6. *Close-eyes-and-describe game.* This will help make family members more consistently aware of their surroundings. Form a family tradition of spontaneously asking a child (or she can ask you) to close her eyes tight and describe what is around her. Play the game whenever you are in a new place to see how much of the environment has been observed. If you are eating in a restaurant, for example, ask someone (without preparation) to close his or her eyes and describe the carpet, wallpaper, lighting, waitress, plates and utensils, table, and so on.

7. *Looking into eyes.* This technique is designed to help children begin to learn the art of observing feelings. Teach your children that the very most interesting place to watch and look is into someone else's eyes. The eye really

is the window to the soul, and those who learn to look directly into the eyes of others tend to observe more about other people and to be less self-aware and self-conscious. Start a family tradition of looking at each other's eyes when you talk and in any one-on-one conversation.

8. Interesting-things game. This is meant to encourage children to observe—and to share what they observe. At the dinner table, or at some opportune time, take turns thinking back and relating the most interesting thing you saw during the day.

Another variation is to have a book of blank paper at some prominent place in the home, called an interest book. Instead of interest on money, the book is for interest in the world around us. Any family member, upon noticing something interesting, can write a sentence or two about it in the interest book. Other family members, especially when feeling bored, can pick up the book and read about some "discoveries." Some sample entries from our interest book include:

> Today I found that mud sticks like glew. (Shawni, at age seven)

> Blossoms—big ones are on the little pear tree we planted in the front yard last year. (Josh, at age ten)

> I got the first kick today from little number six. It's always so exciting! (pregnant Mommy)

> Sunshine make everything look beautiful even baked potatoes, tin foil, hair, glasses, broccoli, and plants. (Saren, at age eight)

> A tennis ball makes a drum noise on the coffee table and makes baby Jonah happy and laugh. (Saren, at age eleven)

I used to think the orange highway markers were witches' hats. (Saydi, at age six)

I used to think that the dog doctor was going to be a dog. (Josh, at age seven)

9. *Mirror-window game*. This game can impress children with how different the world looks when we are more aware of others than of ourselves. You may be able to purchase from a glass store a small piece of one-way glass that is either a mirror or a window, depending on the light. Using such a piece of glass, or alternatively, an empty picture frame or window frame that you can see through, play the following game:

Hold the glass (or frame) up in front of a family member's eyes so that he sees a person. Ask him to describe the person, what he is doing, what it looks like he wants, and so on. Then pretend that the glass (or the frame) is a mirror instead of a window. Have the person describe what he sees now (himself).

Point out that we can't have it both ways. We either see ourselves or we see others. We can't be observant if we are thinking about ourselves. We will miss much of the beauty in the world (as well as the chance to help others and make them happy) if our glass is always a mirror.

Those who see through windows are a force of nature, a force for good, a force that enjoys life and helps others to do the same.

10. *Perspective trips*. These are for the purpose of increasing a child's opportunities to observe. As time and resources allow, travel with your children. Trips need not be long or expensive to accomplish the purpose of giving children a broader perspective. Children who grow up in the same place and never travel may have the advantage of security and "roots," but they also have the disadvantage of limited perspective and of getting the impression that "all the world is just like this." Take a trip to another state, country, or neighborhood. Remember that you can also "travel" through books.

As you travel, make observation and conversation your goals. Notice new things, new ways of doing things, different styles.

11. *Your own methods.* Take a few moments to think of other ideas that would teach your children to be more observant. List them here:

12. *Postquiz.* This will help children review and reinforce what they have learned. At the first meeting of the new month, retake the quizzes you have saved, using the right side of the page for your answers. If your family has explored most of the children's exercises during the month, you will find that your children do far better on the test than they did at the beginning of the month.

Then talk about the need to continue to observe and be aware even as you shift to next month's goal. Discuss the family focal point that follows as a way of continuing to practice what you have learned.

Family Focal Point—Writing

It is not only adults who improve their powers of observation by attempts at poetry or other creative writing. When they are given the opportunity (along with praise and encouragement), children can come up with remarkable observations that lead to equally remarkable poems.

Explain to children that poems do not have to rhyme, that they merely need to express something they have noticed. Show them a poetic attempt or two of your own and encourage them to try. Once they do, give generous praise.

Following a discussion about *really* seeing things that we often pass by and take for granted, our ten-year-old Joshua wrote the following poem after a drive through one of our nearby canyons in late autumn.

PARLEY'S CANYON

Red, orange, yellow and green leaves
Fluttering in the breeze
Happy rivers of color
Flowing down in joy
They mix
Into a beautiful lake of color
Which lets everyone see its joyness.

Since then, we have tried to encourage each child to attempt a short poem at least once a month. Since their efforts are always delightful (and sometimes profound), it is a natural time to *praise* children for their abilities to *observe* as well as for their expressiveness in writing.

Set aside a special place on a family bulletin board or on the refrigerator to display any attempts at poetry or other creative writing.

Whenever a child observes something new or notices something he has never seen before, *use* the occasion to praise him, to reinforce what a good observer he is, and to invite him to write a short poem about it.

Summary

Not many people in the world are consciously or intentionally self-centered. We are not generally insensitive or selfish because we intend to be that way or because we do not wish to be better.

The reason we do not do more for other people is that we don't *think* about it. The reason we don't think is because we don't *see* the needs or the opportunities that are there. If we could see what was needed in a given situation and if we could see what needed to be done to help, we would probably do it.

But we are isolated by not seeing—by our unawareness—and by the self-centeredness that not only makes it hard to see but makes us unhappy and self-worried at the same time.

The unawareness often causes us to look back with regret and think the kind of thoughts that American author Mary Carolyn Davies expressed in her poem:

If I had known what trouble you were bearing
What griefs were in the silence of your face;
I would have been more gentle and more caring,
And tried to give you gladness for a space,
If I had known.

Seeing, then, is the first step, the first skill to be mastered in the equation of sensitivity. We can *train* ourselves and our children to observe. We get good at it by practicing it. As it becomes a more natural part of us, we can progress to the next level of seeing, which involves listening and visualizing and understanding what is beneath the things that we see.

Listening

Those who are quick in talking are not always quick in listening. Sometimes even their brilliance produces a kind of stupidity.

—G. K. CHESTERTON

No man really becomes a fool until he stops asking questions.

—CHARLES P. STEINHOLTZ

The best thing about paying attention to others is that it removes your attention from yourself.

—ANONYMOUS

Illustrations and Stories

We had spent several days in the wilderness of the Umatilla Forest in eastern Oregon, and had observed nature in its most pristine and undisturbed form, sharpening our awareness, as the previous chapter of this book recommends.

Returning to civilization and again surrounded by the noise, the demands, and the judgments of everyday life, we were trying to observe people in the same way we had observed nature. We found it difficult. Unlike nature, the important and meaningful things in people lie *beneath* the surface, and it takes more than sharp eyes to see them.

When you're looking at rocks or trees or mountains, they stay put and invite you to spend as long as you wish looking and understanding. People don't stand still at all. They move, their emotions change, their needs evolve, and they may intentionally not show you on the outside what they are feeling on the inside.

We were discussing these differences on the day we returned from our retreat. We decided that the landscape of a personality is much more difficult to observe than that of a forest or a mountainside.

Seeing people is actually a multisensory activity. We can literally see people, but we can also access them with our ears, and with the inner eyes that allow us to visualize what is beneath the surface.

The questions we ask and the interest we show are like the robot arms and pinchers that grasp a subject and turn it different ways, allowing us to view it from various angles and to perceive what it really is and what it contains. Our ears and our thought receptors are like the microscope through which we take in information and zoom in for a closer look.

When I (Linda) was a typical thirteen-year-old, awkward and self-conscious, I decided one weekend not to attend the school dance. I had no one to go with, I insisted, and would feel embarrassed and self-conscious.

My caring mother gave me a challenge: "Go to the dance and look for someone who feels more self-conscious and ill at ease than you do. There *will* be someone! When you find him or her, introduce yourself and start asking questions until you two become friends and solve each other's problem."

A part of me deeply wanted to go to the dance anyway, so I took the challenge, and found someone, and asked questions, and listened. It worked! I made a friend, and learned one of the most important lessons of my life!

Approaches for Parents

1. Altering social habits. As we seek to improve our own listening skills (so that we can be effective in teaching the same abilities to our children), we might first concentrate on some of our social habits.

Much of the socializing we do consists either of small talk, where the objective is just to keep the conversation going and avoid awkward silences, or of "impressing," where most of what we say is designed to enhance the other person's opinion of us.

If these habits can be altered, great benefits are available. The following three guidelines can help.

ASK AND LISTEN: Look for areas of interest—areas where another person has expertise and you have interest. Ask, and let one question lead to another. While you are learning, the other person will be flattered by your interest and your attention.

PRAISE AND COMPLIMENT: As you listen, look for things you genuinely admire or like. When you find one, mention it. A specific, relevant compliment is often the most valuable thing we can give someone.

SMILE . . . AND REMEMBER NAMES: A smile is the most easy and natural way to tell someone you like him or her. And someone's own name is the most important word in the universe to that person. When you meet someone, repeat his or her name three times in your conversation. Then write it down as soon as you part company. Review and remember all the new names you've collected at the end of each week, fixing them in your permanent memory.

Develop these three habits in dealing with your *children* as well as with your friends.

2. *Active listening, or Rogerian technique.* Children, and adults, for that matter, will tell you a remarkable amount of important and personal things if you *let* them. In most conversations (and particularly those with our children), we are too directive. We ask about this or that (our own interests) and fail to let the person get to *his* or *her* interests.

Active listening (sometimes called Rogerian after the pioneering psychologist Carl Rogers) is a listening tool. By repeating what people have said (in your own words), you reinforce the sense that you have heard them and are interested. You listen with your eyes and body, too, tuned in, focused on the person and on what he or she is saying.

People will go on and on when our listening gives them a secure, "nourished" feeling, and what they say will often be much more interesting (and give you much more insight into them) than what they would say if you were determining the direction of the conversation.

With children the technique is particularly effective. Just say, "Mmm" or "I see" or "So, in other words, you just didn't feel good about it," or whatever you can to demonstrate that you are really hearing. They will go on and on, eventually telling you all you wanted to know and more.

3. A listening-oriented-argument technique. Next time you are embroiled in an argument with your spouse or someone close to you, try this: Have a rule that before you can make your next point, you must repeat or restate his last point accurately enough that he will agree that it was his point. Having done that, you may return to your side of the argument and state your next point. You will find that the argument is defused and that you suddenly understand each other.

Use the same rule when you are debating with one of your children.

4. Relationship goals—relationship descriptions. Most of us assume that even though our relationships are the most important part of our lives, we can't really set goals for them in quite the same way as we set goals for the things we want to *do* and *achieve*.

The fact is, however, that we can set relationship goals in much the same way as we set achievement goals. For both the key is "beginning with the end in mind." With a "people goal" we can sit down and describe a future relationship that we want to have. We can visualize it, study its components, fix it in our minds. We can "see" in our minds a relationship that involves *listening*. Then we can go out and make the vision into reality.

Try sitting down with pen in hand and visualizing the relationship you want in five years with your seven-year-old son, who will then be twelve. Describe on paper what you visualize, how you see yourself listening and understanding. Read the description over every month or so, and gradually it will "program" you right into the relationship you want to have.

A relationship description can take various forms, both in style and in content. One that you write may be very similar or very dissimilar to the two brief excerpts that follow. The first is an excerpt from Linda's description of the relationship she hoped to have with Saren—who was then twelve—at age seventeen. The second is an excerpt from Richard's journal, where he described the relationship he hoped to have with Josh—who was then six—at age eleven.

> *Saren:* When Saren is seventeen, I suspect that she will probably be the same kind of strong-willed person that she was as a child. Coupled with my own strong will, I can foresee sparks flying. However, I can also visualize our conflicts as "debates" rather than "arguments"—where we each really listen to the other. I see myself losing the debate as often as I win it. In debate situations that are not life-and-death issues I can see myself stating my opinion and then encouraging her to make her own decisions (and then standing by them no matter how much it hurts). I bet I'll find she's really right about as often as I am!
>
> More importantly, however, I see Saren becoming one of my best friends by the time she is seventeen. She is intellectually very bright and fun to talk to, so I look forward to times when we can really communicate about things that matter. Because she loves drama, music, and art, I expect we will be able to discuss these things and experience them together. I see our relationship as moving from vertical (parent and child) to horizontal (friend to friend).
>
> *Josh:* Josh is now eleven! We are fishing together on the South Fork. We enjoy being together and feel a sense of

mutual pride in each other. The fish aren't biting, so we've got plenty of time to talk. Josh tells me about a problem he has at school, and I listen, letting him know that I understand and sympathize with what he's saying. I tell him of a similar worry I remember having at about his age.

There is a feeling of trust between us. Josh senses that I love him unconditionally and that nothing he could do would change that. He knows I'll take the time to listen to whatever he wants to say to me.

5. The detective game. So many social occasions these days tend to function only at a superficial level. People talk about the weather or gossip about other people.

An enjoyable way to break this trend when you attend any function as a couple is to have a contest between yourselves to see who can accumulate the most information about any of the other people in attendance. To win, you have to be a better "questioner" and a better listener than your spouse. Each spouse attempts to ask the kind of question that gets him or her into whatever the real interest is of the person he or she is talking with. Once that level is reached, there is much to be learned.

After the function, on the way home, husband and wife can compare notes, telling each other what they learned about what (and about whom), and see who found out the most.

6. Taking notes. Anyone who has ever made the attempt to be a serious student knows how much careful note taking can enhance, improve, and preserve his or her listening ability.

If you could take notes in your personal conversations, you would probably ask better questions and remember much more of what you heard. Well, you can! Or at least you almost can. What you can do immediately after a conversation, as soon as you have a moment, is to make a note or two on a pad.

Whenever you meet a new person, as soon as possible after parting company, jot down his or her name. When you learn something interesting about someone, or when your listening informs you of any new or significant fact, do the same.

If you use a Day-timer or appointment book, try to put whatever notes you make on the day and the time when the conversation happened.

Here is the interesting point: Studies have shown that any form of new information, when reviewed twelve to twenty-four hours after it has been learned, will stay in one's mind approximately ten times longer than if it is never reviewed. This applies to notes we make about people; one review several hours after obtaining it will lock it permanently in the memory.

7. *Your own methods.* Pause for a moment and write down any additional ways or techniques you can think of that would help you hone your own personal listening skills.

Exercises to Teach Children

1. First-Sunday discussion. As before, the purpose of this activity is to interest your children and to get them involved, to make them aware of the goal, and to help them focus on the objectives of the month ahead. By now your children are aware of the objective of developing a new sensitivity skill each month. They need to perceive that you, their parent, are working on these skills yourself—that it is a team project and that you are a "learner" with them.

They also need to realize how valuable and useful these skills are.

Begin your discussion by asking the children if they can think of some advantages or benefits that come from being an excellent listener. They may come up with things such as:

- It will raise your grades in school
- It will win you new friends and make your existing friends like you more
- It will make every day more interesting
- It will make you less self-conscious
- It will give you chances to help other people
- It will make you a good conversationalist, someone that others like to be around

- It will help you in your occupation, no matter what kind of work you choose.

Point out that all of these things are benefits both to you and to other people around you.

2. Prequiz. Let each family member answer the following on the left-hand half of a divided sheet of paper (again, these questions will work as a written quiz for most kids age eight or older. With younger children, just hold a short discussion and adapt the questions to their level):

- What questions do you remember asking during the past month?
- What are the names of persons you tried hard to listen to during the past month?
- What do we listen with?
- How can you get someone else to "really talk" to you?
- Whom did you learn something from this month?
- Did you discover a need that anyone had this month by listening to them?
- Do you have any clear pictures in your mind right now of something you want to do or of something you want to be?

At our first-Sunday meeting on listening we had the children write down reasons for listening. They started out with statements such as: "If you listen, you won't get hit by a train," but progressed to more sophisticated reasons for listening. They wrote, "Listening carefully will: (a) help you do better on tests; (b) let your friends know you are really interested in them, which in turn will; (c) make you more popular; and (d) help you not think so much about yourself."

3. Question game. This helps to focus attention on questions and on the skill and enjoyment of asking them. Occasionally, when you are in a conversation with your children (at dinner, riding in the car, and the like), play the question game. You mention a topic and see who can ask the best question on that topic. (What's the best question you can think of about *bread*? about *clouds*?) Choose topics that are relevant to the moment and praise every question that is asked, particularly the thoughtful, difficult ones.

Explain when you get the chance that asking good questions is even more important and relevant to learning and education than giving good answers. Our schools are too often based on "true-false," "multiple choice," and "one right answer." Kids who never learn how to probe, how to ask good questions, how to discover, are not really educated.

Children should realize that questions are also the tools by which we get to know others and discover their interests, their talents, and their needs.

When children think hard enough about a topic to ask a difficult question about it, they become interested— often so interested that they will amaze you by actually looking for the answer in an encyclopedia or some other rarely used source.

One effective variation on the question game is to have the topic be a feeling (such as loneliness, discouragement, or enthusiasm) or to hold up a picture that expresses an emotion and have the children pose questions that they would want to ask the pictured person. Such a variation is a good preparation for the upcoming objectives of feelings and empathy.

4. *Listening game.* This game is designed to help children recognize that listening is a learned skill. Tell a story or situation or experience involving as many details as you can think of (but not more than *you* can remember). Then ask about those details one at a time and see who has been the best listener.

5. *"What could you learn from that person?"* This exercise is meant to teach children a new way of looking at people. Get in the habit, whenever you are with your children, to point out someone (on the street, in stores, on various jobs) and to ask, "What might you be able to learn from that person? If you could ask that person just one question, what would it be?" (Our four-year-old usually asks, "Where do you sleep?")

6. *Twenty questions.* This is an old, well-known game that can help hone children's analytical-questioning skills. One person thinks of some object or thing known to both players and tells whether it is "animal," "vegetable," or "mineral." The other player has twenty yes-or-no questions to determine what it is. This game teaches children to ask carefully thought-out questions that narrow the field of possibilities. (e.g., "Is it in America? Is it east of the Mississippi?")

7. *Looking-and-listening-for-needs game.* This game can help children begin focusing the seeing and listening skills on opportunities for service. Tell them that this game is an extension of the "observing noses" game you played last month, only this time we'll be looking not at people's *noses* but at their *needs*. Explain that needs are a lot harder to see than noses. To see needs, you have to look hard and listen hard. Someone might just be feeling a little discouraged and need some encouragement, or a little insecure and need a compliment. Or someone might feel left out and need a friend, or might feel useless and need to be asked to help. Or there might be more obvious needs as in the case of a hungry child or a lonely older person.

Select a day for the game, a day when you can be together for dinner in the evening. During the day keep track of how many needs you can notice and identify. Take notes. At dinner that night report on, discuss, and compare those notes.

8. *Argument technique.* This is meant to teach listening skills at the same time that you solve arguments. Adapt the number-three point under "Approaches for Parents" in this chapter to your kids: before a new point is made, the last stated position has to be repeated.

9. *The one-two punch of compliment and question: putting people at ease.* This experience can help children understand one of the purposes of asking good questions. Both through your example and through any discussion you can muster, help children see that they can put others at ease by asking good, relevant questions of people and by finding some small thing on which to compliment them. Explain that an important skill in life is putting people at ease so that they can be relaxed and talk openly about what they feel. Give some examples of how interest-showing questions and a thoughtful compliment can accomplish this.

We managed to capture our children's interest on this point by presenting the concept in the form of an equation:

$$Q + C = AE$$

Without any explanation we put the equation on a piece of paper one day and taped it to the wall where it would get noticed. When someone asked what it meant, we explained (Questions + Compliments = At Ease) and told them that it was a skill we were trying to learn. Predictably they asked if they could work on it too.

10. *Your own methods.* Take a few moments and think about what other things you could do to teach the skills of listening. Think hard—ideas will come. List them:

11. *Postquiz.* With this exercise you review and reinforce what has been learned. On the "first-Sunday" that ends this "month," retake the test from the beginning of the month and then discuss the progress everyone has made in becoming good listeners and questioners.

Family Focal Point—The Icebreaker Award

The Icebreaker Award can regularly encourage and reward children in their efforts to ask and listen. Few things give genuine recognition and praise as clearly and strongly as an award. Children of any age, right through the teenage years, tend to do over again what they are recognized for and what they receive attention for.

The awards discussed here are not money, toys, or candy. Rather they are praise, recognition, and attention in the form of a little certificate or plaque that can be put on a child's door to reinforce and recognize a particular form of desirable behavior.

Of course awards are most gratifying when presented at an assembly before a large audience (which we have right in our home when all eleven of us sit around the dinner table). However, presentation of this type of award works just as effectively with one or two children.

This first award consists of a large *I.B.*, lettered on construction paper and mounted on cardboard. After Sunday dinner we ask, "Who is in the running for the Icebreaker Award? Children think back over the week and remember the times they took the conversation initiative and asked good questions in their efforts to get to know others. Whoever can tell of the best instance of listening and asking the kind of questions that gave him insights and information about the person he was speaking to wins the award and posts it on his bedroom door for the coming week. Parents should be in the running too. There can be a tie—or more than one winner.

The real benefit of this award ceremony lies in the discussion and in everyone's efforts to think back and recall his or her own efforts to ask and listen.

Summary

Asking and listening is a form of analysis, a form of exploration, a form of discovery! And it is the most exciting form. Through our questions and interest we collect the "specimens" of information and insight, put them on slides, and prep them for a closer look. Our listening is the microscope through which we become aware and in tune.

A listener is a *learner*. And a listener is fulfilling one of the prerequisites of sensitivity.

Feeling

No matter how accurately we see or how well we listen, we know little of sensitivity until we can perceive and understand feelings—both our own and those of others. Three related qualities are involved:

- *Congruence,* which we will define as the ability both to know and to admit how *you* feel

- *Concern,* which involves taking that same level of interest in the feelings of the people you are with

- *Empathy,* which implies an extension of this same concern to those you are not with or have not met

Together congruence, concern, and empathy are the threads in the emotional fabric of sensitivity.

UNDERSTANDING

OBSERVING

FEELING

COMMUNICATING

+ DOING

= SENSITIVITY

Congruence:
"How Do I Feel?"

He who has such little knowledge of human value as to seek happiness by changing anything but his own disposition will waste his life in fruitless efforts and multiply the grief he proposes to remove.

—Samuel Johnson

As important as it is to observe and understand what is outside of ourselves, the more important realities are within . . . and they are our feelings.

Illustrations and Stories

The awareness that makes sensitivity possible is not accomplished by seeing and listening only. No matter how good we become at those skills, they are not by themselves enough.

The kind of true, inner awareness that leads to genuine empathy and sensitivity also requires feelings that are both accurate and perceptive. The spur of service, the energy of empathy, and the catalyst of charity are *feelings*.

Feelings are not vague, whimsical, unreliable imaginings. They are our most trusted and honest sense. Our eyes can trick us, and we often hear things that are not really there, but deep and true feelings never lie, and they carry with them our greatest insights into ourselves and others.

Before we can become very good at empathizing and knowing how others feel, we must develop and perfect our ability to know how we ourselves are feeling. We are congruent if we can honestly interpret our own feelings, so that what we *do* and *say* matches perfectly with what we actually *feel*. If we can be that congruent within ourselves, then we can become better at understanding how other people feel.

Teddy Roosevelt said that the place he would least like to be was "among those cold and timid souls who never knew either victory or defeat." He, like most of us, wanted to be among those who dare to live and dare to feel!

We once had a friend who seemed to take everything literally. When someone said, "How are you?" he took it as a real question wanting a real answer. His real answer usually took five minutes or so (at least four and a half minutes longer than most people wanted to hear). He told of his physical health, of his moods as of late, of his family, even of his finances.

We may not want to reevaluate every facet of "how we are" whenever someone asks, but we do need to know those answers within ourselves. We need both to know and to be able to express how we feel. For as we get to know our feelings, we get to know ourselves!

Here is a poem written by Saydi (at age ten) that seems to express exactly how she felt:

WHO AM I?

Who am I?
To my parents I'm a child,
Who they care for and love.
And to my teacher
A person who knows not the answer
And when I ask a question says only, "You decide."
To strangers I'm
A person who has blue eyes
And brown hair
And is called a strange name: Saydi.
I'm a target to my enemies
And I'm a friend to my friends.
Well, to my brothers, I'm nice
But they do say I yell a lot.
To my sisters I'm a slob,
And a weird person.
What's amazing is that they don't understand
Why I do things.
Oh well . . . to myself
I'm mature and alert and try to finish
The puzzle.
I'm a person who loves children
And wants to be a mom.
I sometimes dream about bad things.
Sometimes my bedtimes and parents
Make me want to run away.
I always remember good times and forget the bad.
I like to dance
But it wears me out.
So does finding the success of my life!

We were impressed with the story we heard from some parents about their thirteen-year-old son. He and his younger sister had had a disagreement over who got to use the home computer one evening and the boy had slapped her. The father grabbed him by the shoulders and demanded, "Why did you do that, son?"

Now, that's usually not a very good question to ask children, particularly younger ones. We will ask something like, "Why did you pour out that cereal?" and of course the kid doesn't know why he did it.

But with this boy the question was more meaningful. The father really did wonder why he had done it, and so did the boy. He was not usually physical, especially with his sister. No answer came to him, though, and he only said, "I'm sorry."

About an hour later the boy came to his dad and said, "I've been thinking about your question and I think I know the answer."

The father looked at his son, obviously proud of him, and asked him to go on.

"Well," said the boy, "I went to my room to think about it, and I remembered that my math teacher embarrassed me in front of the whole class today. I was so mad at her, but I couldn't do anything about it, so I just kept all those bad feelings inside of me all day. I think I just let them out at Sis." Children are often remarkably good at talking about how they feel—and even at knowing why they feel that way. And they get better at it if we praise their every attempt and ask them often, "How do you feel?"

When you stop to think about it, most of our ultimate goals are *feeling* goals. We want to be happy, we want to be fulfilled, we want to be loved, we want to be kind, we want to have inner peace. All these goals are feelings. We may say we want to earn money, to build a new house, to finish college—but these are all secondary goals. The *reason* we want the money or the house or the college degree is because we believe it will make us happier, because it will make us feel better!

The best thing to say, then, when we first open our eyes in the morning, is "What can I feel today?" and "How can I enjoy these feelings?" If it's a day filled with work responsibilities and difficult tasks, we can derive feelings of accomplishment, completion, even purposeful fatigue. If it is a day of relaxation, we can derive feelings of rejuvenation and peace. If it's just a routine, drab, ordinary day, we can resolve to observe more and notice more, thus deriving feelings of interest and appreciation.

Memories are not years or days. Memories are *moments*. Memories are not sighs or sounds. Memories are *feelings*.

We were cross-country skiing on a sparkling white and blue and golden Saturday. As we glided along, stretching our legs, pushing our poles, huffing our steamy breath, there was a sense of simple elation. "You know," Linda puffed, "this is a pretty good 'now.' "

Since then we have used that phrase often. Sitting around the dinner table enjoying each other's company, enjoying a conversation with friends, watching a sunset, peeking in on a sweet, sleeping child—one of us will look at the other and say, "This is a pretty good 'now.' "

Learning to identify, recognize, and appreciate feelings within ourselves is good training for appreciating the now.

Don't brush off this notion. Don't say, "Well, I think I already know how I feel." Most of us don't . . . most of the time. We don't have an accurate or complete sense of how we feel in those very rare moments when we are stricken with extreme sadness or filled with intense excitement. But most of the time we just feel "fine," or "okay," or "all right, I guess," or as the British always say, "not too bad."

It is a skill to be more consistently in tune with how you feel. To do so, you must be honest—honest with yourself.

There is nothing that gives you more control over your feelings than being able to identify them. "I feel a little bit jealous of Frank." "I feel kind of proud of myself for fixing that thermostat." "I feel intense frustration when the boss asks me to stay for these late meetings."

Just knowing or identifying a feeling sometimes makes it your friend rather than your enemy. And once you're acquainted with it, it's easier to ask the feeling either to stay or to leave.

If our goal is to teach our children sensitivity, then the subject matter of the course really is feelings. The place to start is with our own feelings. Once we have a handle on those, we can use them like a net to "catch" the feelings of others.

The novelist Storm Jameson said that happiness came not from comfort but from the capacities "to enjoy simple things, to think freely, to feel deeply, to risk life, to be needed."

Of her five capacities, the middle one—to feel deeply—is the fulcrum for all the others. Each of the other four produce happiness only as they create within us deep feelings.

Approaches for Parents

1. Be real. We ought to learn to drop our facades and be honest about our feelings to ourselves as well as our children. Usually the clear expression of real feelings benefits all concerned. By articulating what they are feeling, parents learn to know themselves and also depressurize their emotions by talking about them. As children hear their parents discuss their feelings, they become reassured of their parents' honesty and of the fact that their own feelings are okay and need not be hidden or suppressed.

Often the best way we can respond to our children is to express how we feel. Instead of saying to a child, "You're bad for doing this," "or "You're good for doing that," we might say, "I feel upset when you do this," or "It makes me feel so good to see you do that."

Any alternative to being honest about your feelings can create a troublesome artificial feeling that undermines trust. Imagine a father, for example, who tries too hard always to act as if he were calm, when he is in fact highly upset, even livid. This type of parent, when one of his small children has done something flagrantly naughty, takes him into his den and says (as he grits his teeth), "Now, Johnny, Daddy's not mad, but you're going to have to have a little spanking for what you did."

It's more honest to say, "Johnny, I feel very upset at what you did. In fact I feel so upset by it that I think we'd both better just sit here for a minute while I calm down before we talk about what the punishment should be."

So, as usual, approach number one is to set the example! Try hard to recognize and identify your real feelings and to express them to your spouse and to your children.

2. Learn to figure out the source of your feelings. As

we practice identifying and expressing our feelings, we also need to work on understanding where they come from. When Mom says, "I feel upset because Billy spilled his milk on my one good tablecloth and he's old enough to be more careful," she might want to ask herself why that upset her so much more than when the same thing happened last week. She might find that it's the fact that the checkbook didn't balance that really upsets her and that Billy's milk just "triggered" the latent feeling.

Trying to identify the real source of feelings also helps us to be more accurate in naming and expressing them. For example, you might say in the foregoing situation, "I feel really upset because I had some frustrations with my checkbook, and now I've got this mess to clean up."

3. *Separate negative feelings about behavior from sensitive love for the child.* It is so important to be aware of this differentiation and to make it clear to children. Sometimes the best way to be aware of it is to say it as simply as possible, "I love you, Jennifer, but I don't like at all what you just did!"

4. *Be open and candid about positive feelings.* Frustration, anger, and irritation are not the only feelings we ought to be honest about. The positive feelings of pride, love, and concern should be expressed with equal honesty (instead of taken for granted and not mentioned).

When a child does well, gives something a good try, or exhibits any other good behavior, we should take every opportunity to tell the child how good that makes us feel. Say, "I feel so happy when I see you sharing with your sister," or "It makes me feel proud and excited when I see a test paper like that."

This type of "I feel" expression is often better than saying, "You are so smart in math." Children need to

draw their own conclusions about themselves, and knowing how *they* made *you* feel will help greatly in this
process.

Perhaps the most important place of all to be real and
genuine is in the love we show for our children *after* we
have disciplined them or shown our disfavor with something they have done. If we're not careful, children begin
to perceive parents as their enemies, or at least as barriers
to what they want to do and as constant critics who are
forever disciplining, correcting, and finding things to be
displeased with. But when parents make a conscious effort
to express love after disciplining, it "completes the circle,"
making it very clear that it was the behavior that the parent was displeased with and that no behavior could ever
dilute the love the parent has for the child.

*5. After recognizing and expressing feelings, learn
how to alter them.* Norman Cousins, whose book
Anatomy of an Illness tracked his own battle with a life-
threatening disease, concluded that the mind can control
what goes on in the body, even the correction of sickness.
Cousins believed the body is a "walking apothecary,"
which can release any number of different chemicals into
the bloodstream, thus altering both a person's physical
condition and how he or she feels.

Feelings are often a somewhat complex combination of
the psychological, the mental, and the emotional person—
and of the situation in which the person finds himself or
herself. Thus we can change how we feel either by changing our situation or by changing something within us.

Many times, however, it is easier to change ourselves
than to change our situation. We all hear of people who
become experts in meditation, practice relaxation techniques, exercise or do aerobics, take a brief nap, or pray

briefly but deeply. Apparently each of these can substantially alter the mental state, releasing certain chemicals into the bloodstream and changing very dramatically how we feel.

Each of us ought to find our own way of consciously altering or changing the way we feel so that we do not have to endure damaging and dangerous negative moods or depression for any long periods of time.

6. Appreciate our "moods" and realize that most, if not all, of them have a positive side. Our goal to be able to change how we feel should not extend to the point of wanting always to feel happy, optimistic, and outgoing. Everyone needs pensive times, quiet times, times for reflection, for reevaluation, even for sadness and worry.

All of these feelings have their uses. It is often in our deeper and perhaps less pleasant periods that we resolve to improve, search our hearts for real purpose and meaning, and become sensitive to the needs and feelings of others.

And there is something worse than feeling bad. It is not feeling at all. The real goal to be worked toward this month is to feel more and to be more aware and more able to define and talk about what we feel.

Perhaps no feeling is inherently bad. It's just that some feelings often manifest themselves in negative ways. One might think, for example, of loneliness as a "bad" feeling, yet it could, if handled right, provide a time to reflect and also be the motivation for greater friendliness and more social effort. Anger, if controlled, could produce positive change, as could frustration or even disillusionment.

Practice this month learning to: (a) ask yourself how you feel; (b) answer this question to yourself; (c) find the positive aspects of that feeling and appreciate them; and

(d) identify the negative aspects of the feeling and try to get rid of them.

7. *Relish those moments when we feel moved.* What happens when we hear an emotionally beautiful piece of music, or watch a performance of excellence, or hear a touching story or poem that brings tears to our eyes? A thrill goes down the spine; we feel a tingling sensation; a lump comes to the throat, moisture to the eye.

We all love to be moved because it is the deepest of feelings. And that thought reinforces the goal of this month—to better recognize, better define, and deepen our own feelings.

8. *Your own methods.* Take a few minutes and list any other approaches or methods you can think of to make yourself more aware and more appreciative of your own feelings:

Exercises to Teach Children

1. First-Sunday discussion. This activity is intended to firmly establish in everyone's mind the objective for the month ahead of becoming more aware of his or her own feelings. As usual with a new month, begin with a discussion that involves your children. Adjust it for their ages and build it around the following points:

- How important are feelings? And how real are they? In a way feelings are more real than anything else because what we feel is what we are! And sometimes feelings are more reliable than any other sense. Our eyes can trick us, and our ears, too, but our deepest feelings, if we can identify them and know them, will never lie to us.

  (Note: At this point in our family meeting, our thirteen-year-old recalled the times she "thought she saw something"—the water mirages on the road, the shapes in the dark trees behind our house. The eleven-year-old remembered a trip when she heard a growling lion in the hotel room next to ours, which turned out to be the loud snoring of a very large man. Then we talked about feelings, particularly feelings of love—and about how *sure* and how *real* they are.)

- Why it is important to be aware of our feelings and to try to know why we feel the way we do. If we can identify our feelings and their sources, we can appreciate them, we can control them better, and we can begin to develop the ability to tell how others feel as well.

- Talk about goals for the month ahead: We're going

to try to think more about how we feel, to tell each other how we feel, to identify and name our feelings.

2. Prequiz. As usual in opening a month, have everyone (including parents) take a brief test in the left-hand column of a divided piece of paper.

(Note: By the time we began this third month in our family, the children had become somewhat used to the idea of taking a test that would be rather hard at the beginning of a month and much easier when they retook it at the end. The tests had become a way of helping them look forward to the skill we would be working on and a means of keeping their minds on that skill so that they *would* do better on the retake.)

- Name as many different feelings or kinds of emotions that you have experienced during the month just passed.
- Pick out one feeling you remember having and explain why you felt that way—what caused you to feel the way you felt?
- Would it be good if we could always feel happy—if we could get rid of all the other feelings? Why or why not?

3. Use the word feel—*both in telling and in asking.* This activity can to help children become more generally aware of your feelings and of theirs. As you form the habit of saying "I feel," also form the habit of asking "How do you feel?"

Move away from asking children so many why, when, and where questions and start asking more "how do you feel about" questions.

Encourage children to identify their feelings and express them to you, and praise every effort they make to
talk about their feelings.

4. *Family storytelling*. Working with this technique
your children can use stories about relatives as case studies
to identify feelings. If you have any stories or histories of
grandparents or ancestors (perhaps in old diaries or journals or perhaps passed on verbally by your parents), you
are well prepared to ask your children to describe the feelings they think a certain ancestor had in a particular situation. Trying to describe these imagined feelings (verbally
or in writing) also serves as a bridge into the following
two chapters, which attempt to teach children (and ourselves) to focus on the feelings of others instead of on just
their own.

In our family we are fortunate to have a number of
histories, journals, letters, and diaries written by grandparents and ancestors, along with some stories we remembered our parents telling us about their parents. When our
oldest children were still very small, we began to wish for
ways to tell them about these progenitors. We ended up
taking some of the accounts and, without changing the
facts, rewriting them into children's stories and binding
them into a book. This "ancestor book" has become the
children's favorite collection of bedtime stories and has
been a way of "packaging" the sensitivity and character of
some of our ancestors and passing those traits along to the
children as a gift and a heritage.

Three of our children's favorites follow. They may
prompt some memories of personal family stories that you
can pass on to your children.

GRANDPA DAN AND THE CAT THAT CAME BACK

When Grandpa Dan was a very small boy in Sweden, he found a cat. He cared for the cat and loved him. But Dan's family was very poor and they couldn't afford milk or food to feed the cat. Dan's father told him to give the cat away. But every time Dan gave him away, the cat would run back to the Swenson home. That cat loved Dan and would not go to anyone else. Mr. Swenson said the cat *had* to go, so Dan, with tears in his eyes, took the cat far to the other side of the city and tried to leave him. But the cat followed Dan home. Dan could not get rid of him. Finally Dan's father told him to do what seemed like a very terrible thing. He told Dan to put the cat in a big gunnysack, tie a rope around it, tie a rock to the rope, and throw it into the deepest part of the river. Mr. Swenson was not a mean man; he just didn't want the cat to starve and suffer, and this was the only thing he could think of.

Dan was so sad that all he could do was cry. But he obeyed his father. Mr. Swenson helped tie the bag very tight so that the cat couldn't get out, and he helped tie the big rock to the bag. Sobbing all the way, Dan carried his precious cat to the bridge, nearly a mile away. He closed his eyes and threw the bag and stone in. Then he ran home through the forest, crying as though his little heart would break. As he rounded the last corner and saw his house, Dan couldn't believe his eyes. There, sitting on the front porch with his tail curled around him and licking one front paw . . . was the cat!

When Mr. Swenson found out what had happened, he called Dan in and said, "Dan, that is a remarkable cat. Somehow he got out of the bag and ran home so fast, he was all dry and sunning himself on the porch before you could even run back. I can see how much you love him. If you'll work hard enough to earn a little extra for milk, you can keep him."

GRANDPA DEAN AND THE CAR WRECK

Dean had just earned his driver's license. How excited he was! On Friday he had a date for a dance in the next town—a double date with a friend—and Dean was going to drive!

Everything went fine until they got to the town and drove over a hill. The street was slippery and the car skidded into another car parked in front of the hotel. It must have been late—perhaps it was after the dance—because all of the lights in the hotel were off and they didn't go in or knock.

The cars weren't dented badly, and Dean drove home with a heavy heart. His conscience told him he had to go back and find the owner of the car and figure out a way to pay for the damage. Dean *always* had a strong conscience. He always *knew* what was right and didn't feel good inside until he had done it.

When he got home, he woke up his father. His father was a very good and wise dad. (You know about him—he is Great-grandpa.) He listened to Dean's story and told him that he was proud of him for being honest and following his conscience. They got up very early the next morning and went back to the hotel before anyone else was awake. They found the owner of the damaged car, and Grandpa Great paid to have it fixed. Dean saved the money from his paper route and paid his daddy (Grandpa Great) back. It was quite a lot of money, but Dean felt great inside because he had done the right thing, told the truth, and followed his conscience.

A Hard Life, But Lots of Fun

On October 13, 1905, a sweet little girl was born to Arthur and Ida Clark in the little town of Freedom, Wyoming. She was a dear, good-natured, healthy little child—the third in the family, but she didn't stay "the baby" very long, as her mother had a new baby almost every year until there were ten in all. But this little girl was very special to us because she was named Hazel (and she is your grandmother).

Hazel's life was filled with many happy memories, but her childhood was not easy. Hard work was the key to survival for this big family. Her daddy owned a large farm, and each child had many responsibilities to keep their farm and family going. Boys and girls alike helped to do the sowing and reaping, cooking and diaper changing.

When Hazel was only about six; her brother, Wilford, seven; and her little sister (and best friend), Florence, five, her father built a special box that fit on the farm machinery where they could sit so that they wouldn't fall off, and often left them all day (with their little lunches) to guide the horses as they plowed or harrowed the fields while he worked in another place on the farm.

One of the favorite games in the Clark household was started by Hazel's mother, Ida, and carried on by the children through the years. It was called the "Let's Surprise Father Game." Often they would say, "Let's surprise Father and get all the chores done or the cows milked by the time he gets home."

Thus many times when Father Arthur came home tired and aching from a long day of hard labor on the farm, dreading the never-ending chores of milking the cows, he would only see the delighted looks on his children's faces when they told him it was all done!

School was another interesting adventure in the Clark family and for Hazel and the other school-going children. It meant getting up *very* early in the morning to finish the milking and the other chores before they left. On one or two occasions when all the other family members were sick, Hazel got up at three or four in the morning and milked all twenty-five cows by herself before leaving for school.

Traveling to school was *very* different in those days for Hazel and her brothers and sisters. When Wilford, Hazel, and Florence were only eight, seven, and six, they were all sent to school on one horse. The problem was that there was a river between the house and the school, and to go around it meant a six-mile journey, whereas going through it cut the distance to a mile and a half. They did the inevitable. Holding each other's feet up so that they wouldn't get too wet, they guided the trusty horse as he stumbled through the deep, swift water to the other side every morning and afternoon. In the wintertime they even broke through the ice if it wasn't too thick to get the horse safely through, and often arrived at school cold and soggy.

5. Poetry This idea is used again, as in Month 1, to help children feel their feelings more deeply and understand them by expressing them. As mentioned, few activities affect children's ability to observe (or provide more delight for their parents) than attempts at poetry. For children, as for adults, poetry comes from feelings; attempts to write cause us all to look and think harder about how things feel.

About the time we started Month 3 in our family, our children were taking a poetry class in our home with a group of neighborhood children. The teacher was truly amazing. She had pulled things out of the children's minds that showed a level of seeing and feeling that absolutely astounded us. She did give them word lists to work with (you could use the adjective list from Exercise 9) and poem titles and concepts that they could include, but the poetry was created and written entirely by the children. Some examples follow:

VACATION
BY JOSHUA EYRE (AGE TEN)

Vacation is a bored tiger
getting freed from his nasty cage.
Vacation is a raccoon
freeing itself from
a hunter's trap.
Vacation is your friend
getting out of jail.
Vacation is a tree
letting its leaves and branches
blow free in the cool breeze.
Vacation is playing
my favorite free song
on the piano.

THUNDER
BY SAYDRIA EYRE (AGE EIGHT)

Thunder wanders through your dreams
and sings loud and scary songs
through the night.
It stirs through the dark green plants
then curls up real tight and sleeps.

LONELINESS
BY JOSHUA EYRE (AGE TEN)

Loneliness is a TV set
in an old house
which now is empty.
Loneliness is when
you wake up
in the middle of the night
while everyone is asleep.
Loneliness is you
by yourself on a walk.
That's what I think it is,
do you?

WHAT'S HUNGRY?
BY SAREN EYRE (AGE FOURTEEN)

Wolves are hungry
for the meat of deer.
The wind is hungry
for something to blow
away.
Some people are hungry
for great wealth.
A dry stream bed
is hungry for water.
Winter trees are hungry
for leaves
in the spring.
The world is hungry,
sometimes for war,
sometimes for peace.

WHAT'S HUNGRY?
BY SAYDRIA EYRE (AGE EIGHT)

I'm hungry
you're hungry.
I guess everyone
is hungry.
My room is hungry—
it wants so bad
to be cleaned.
And this poem is hungry
to get finished.

WHAT'S TIRED?
BY SHAWNI EYRE (AGE TWELVE)

A lion is tired
when a yawn comes
to its mouth,
when its huge
sharp teeth
open wide,
and when its mane
droops low.

The sky is tired
when snow blows
from its darkened clouds.

The golden sun is tired
after spreading its rays
to all the earth,
but when dawn comes

they've had rest
and are no longer tired.

6. *Speeches on feelings.* This will give children additional opportunities to concentrate their thoughts on feelings they have experienced. Sometimes a good way to focus our thoughts on something is to give a brief speech about it. At the dinner table ask each family member to give a one-minute speech on a topic such as "How I felt when Dad got home from his business trip," or "How I felt when I didn't make the Pep Club," or "How I felt last Wednesday when I finished my midterm test."

Pick subjects at first where feelings are quite obvious. Later, with some experience, pick subjects where feelings are more subtle and harder to define ("How I felt yesterday afternoon at school") and where kids have to think hard to remember and conclude how they felt.

Be sure *you* participate. Let the children decide on the topic for your speech.

7. *Humor.* This is meant to help children see that a sense of humor can modify their own feelings and also help others to feel better. Get in the habit of thinking (and saying), "Was there anything funny or amusing about it?" Ask the question whenever someone is describing a feeling. Learn to look at the lighter side of things.

There is a formula that says, "Crisis plus time equals humor." And it is true that we look back on some of our biggest frustrations as rather humorous situations. By consciously looking for the lighter side, some of the humor can often come right along with the crisis, and we can teach children how to modify their moodiest moods.

Also encourage the telling of good, wholesome jokes, as well as laughter in general. Observation and listening skills often lead to the *noticing* of something that is ironic or humorous and funny. Take the time to laugh and to encourage laughter. It is the nearest thing we have to a cure-all medicine.

8. *Journals.* This activity is a way to use writing as a vehicle to identify and understand feelings. If there is anything even more useful than poetry in the clarifying of feelings, it is journal writing. As discussed earlier, journals can greatly increase both our observing and our listening abilities. The privacy of a journal makes it an appropriate place to record our deepest feelings, whatever they are.

Encourage children to begin many of the sentences in their journal with the words *I felt* or *I feel.*

9. *Adjective game.* This exercise is designed to assist children in defining their feelings and in increasing their ability to verbalize them. During this month, as a family, make a long list of adjectives that describe how people can feel. Start with the most basic feelings, such as *happy, sad, mad, frustrated, embarrassed,* and according to the ages of your children, move to more specific and interesting adjectives, such as *murky, jumpy, agitated, perplexed, elated.*

Try to list at least one hundred words before you are finished. Explain that a good vocabulary helps us figure out our feelings as well as express them.

Hang the list in a visible place and invite family members to add to it whenever they think of another good adjective or whenever they feel an emotion that is not described by any word on the list.

This list will add another dimension to the speeches or journaling noted in Exercises 6 and 8 in this section and will also be useful whenever the question "how do you feel?" is asked in your family.

10. *Tracing your feelings.* This exercise is intended to

help children identify the sources of their feelings. After any of the foregoing methods that challenge us to define feelings, ask the question "what caused the feeling?" Practice with your children the skill of identifying where feelings started and what factors led to them.

Help children to see the connections between physical things and feelings. For example, if you don't eat breakfast, your blood sugar will be low, and you may be more irritable, or if a woman is pregnant, her hormone balance may shift and rather drastically alter her moods and how she feels.

Tell the two following brief stories to illustrate that feelings can build and can be transferred.

Mr. Raymond had had a bad day at the office. Several of his clients were behind on their payments, and his secretary had to leave early because she was sick. When he came home, he was short-tempered with his wife. Mrs. Raymond felt bad because of how her husband treated her, so she yelled at Billy when he forgot to wipe his feet after school. Billy was upset, so he shoved his sister, Suzy, when she bumped into him in the hallway. Suzy was angry at Billy, so she kicked the dog when he walked in front of her as she went outside. The dog yelped and took a nip at the cat, who was usually his best friend.

Isn't it interesting how a sick secretary can cause a cat to get bitten by a dog?

Charles was walking home from basketball practice one day, dribbling his basketball on the street. The ball hit a sharp piece of glass and developed a slow leak. Charles had just bought the ball three days before. When he got home, his younger sister was in his room. Charles got very upset at his sister, whom he had told never to go into his room without permission.

11. Handling worry. This activity is meant to help children worry less *about* worrying. Explain that there are two basic kinds of worries: the ones we can't do anything about and the ones we can. Have a goal as a family to spend any "worrying time" on the second kind. Point out that there are plenty of things to worry about that you *can* do something about, so there is no point in worrying about the other kind.

12. Your own ideas. List any other ways or means that you think would help your children become better at identifying and understanding their own feelings:

13. Postquiz. On the "first Sunday" of the new month retake the test you started with a month ago in order to review and reinforce what you have learned. Praise everyone for their improvement during the month (which will be illustrated by how much better they will do on this postquiz than they did on the prequiz).

Discuss the benefits and the enjoyment of being more aware of your own feelings, and then move on to the family focal point as a way of staying in the habit of identifying and expressing how you feel.

Family Focal Point—Expressing Feelings

Having a set time when it is easy to share feelings can improve and deepen family communication. Begin the practice of opening your monthly family meetings (before you get to your discussion of next month's topic or the prequiz) by inviting everyone to take a turn standing and expressing his or her feelings. If you, the parent, set the example by standing first and talking briefly about how you feel (your love for spouse and children, the gratitude you feel, the concerns you have), children will follow suit (although more briefly) when it is their turn.

This habit has been very beneficial to our family. Since we do it regularly on the first Sunday of each month, children expect it and even look forward to it. We encourage each child to use the words "I feel" as often as possible and to be completely open and candid and as *accurate* as they can be about their feelings. It is a chance for us as parents to express our love and appreciation to them in a very direct, open way, and it brings us all more in touch with our feelings. In the open atmosphere of this type of meeting, negative feelings sometimes come out, but usually without the sting that they might carry in a less loving atmosphere. Our eleven-year-old illustrated this one month when she said, "I feel a lot of love for you all," and then with a twinkle in her eye, "Saren, too, even though she'll never let me borrow her sweater."

Summary

People who know how they feel and who can be honest both with themselves and with others are people of character and strength. It takes courage to admit feelings to ourselves and to talk about them to others. People who learn to do so will begin to find life's experiences more meaningful, will become more sure of themselves and of their personal dreams and ambitions, and will become far more capable of seeing and identifying the feelings of others—which is the object of our next two "months."

A side benefit of becoming better at understanding what we feel and why is that we grow to think of ourselves as more *responsible* for our feelings, and we gain a measure of confidence in our ability to decide for ourselves how we will feel and how we will think rather than letting other people or outside factors determine our feelings, beliefs, and preferences for us.

The writer S. D. Gordon said, "Shoes define men into three classes. Some men wear their father's shoes. They make no decisions of their own. Some are unthinkingly shod by the crowd. The strong man is his own cobbler. He insists on making his own choices. He walks in his own shoes."

As we progress, we learn that one of the choices we can make relates to how we feel. And we learn that our feelings can be unique and individual, made up of our own attitudes and beliefs as well as the results of "what happens to us." Most importantly we learn that feelings are at the core of people. We first understand ourselves by learning to know our feelings. Then we can attempt to know others by grasping and empathizing with their feelings. That type of grasping and empathizing is the topic of the next two months.

Concern:

"How Do You Feel?"

*"God, let me be aware—stab my soul fiercely
with other's pain."*

—Miriam Teichner

*"One of the sanest, surest and most generous
joys of life comes from being happy over the good
fortune of others."*

—Archibald Rutledge

Illustrations and Stories

The Archibald Rutledge quote that opens this chapter
contains a remarkably simple truth. There are enough moments of pleasure and personal fulfillment in our lives to
keep us always happy, but if we can learn to truly feel the
joys of others, then we can multiply our joy.

The other side of the coin is represented by the Teichner quote. When we are truly empathetic and able to feel
what others feel, we feel the *pain* that they feel as well as
the pleasure.

Both the joy and the pain of others can be great benefits because each expands our experience and teaches us the lessons of life.

If it is true (and it is) that there is no progress "from ease to ease," and if it is true (and it is) that we progress and grow only through challenge and that muscles strengthen only through exercise and use, then we must experience personal crisis, hardship, pain, or despair before we can grow or develop. Right?

Wrong! We *will* all experience some measure of these things and they will be opportunities for learning and for growth. But there are other ways to grow, ways that involve the challenges, crises, and needs of *others*. As we learn to feel the feelings of others, we not only put ourselves in a position to help, we put ourselves in a position to grow.

It is not hard to believe in our ability to feel what others feel. All who have truly loved someone know that it is possible to feel *for* someone. When our children are sick and we feel their pain more than they do, when our spouse is hurt and we wish we could remove the pain by taking it on ourselves—in situations like these we *do*, through our concern, know much of how another person feels.

The skill we should work for is to feel that empathy more commonly and more frequently—to know more accurately how the person we are talking to feels, to be aware on a constant and ongoing basis of the feelings of the person we are dealing with. The literal definition of *sympathy* is "to feel sorry *for* someone."

Children are sometimes remarkably capable of this kind of concern. One day as I was going out the door with seven-year-old Talmadge for a "Mommy date," he asked, "Can Saydi and Jonah come with us?" Surprised at the request because I knew how much he liked being alone with just me on our rare "dates," I said, "Sure, but why do you want them to come?"

"Well, the last time we had a Mommy date they were begging to come and I didn't want them to, so we left them home. They were already out in the car, remember, and you told them to get out because it was my turn to go alone. When we got to the store, I kept begging you to go back because I remembered their sad faces when they got out. This time I want them to come, but they can shop in a different store. That way everybody will be happy."

True maturity means the opposite of selfishness, self-centeredness, and self-consciousness. It is being able to turn the mirrors that surround us into windows.

The poet Angela Morgan, perhaps thinking of this type of mature concern, said, "I will hew great windows, wonderful windows, measureless windows for my soul."

The question of "how do you feel" is not as easy as it sounds. Sometimes we think we know how someone feels because we know how *we* would feel in their shoes. However, sometimes we have to come to grips with the fact that the Golden Rule does not always apply.

When we were first married, I (Linda) remember distinctly learning this lesson when we visited the beautiful home of some older, more established friends. Richard settled down to watch a football game and leisurely rested his feet on the coffee table. The hostess was not pleased. Richard felt sorry to have upset her and insisted (to me, not her) that he was only doing what he would want someone to do in *his* home.

Another example: Whereas my mother would love a surprise visit from a long-lost cousin, I would be embarrassed if she showed up unexpectedly on one of "those days" when things are disheveled everywhere and I'm trying to get a child through a crisis.

We need to consider that people have vastly different perspectives and needs. We need to consider their feelings and try to anticipate what would make them happy, rather than assuming that they are "just like us" and would—or should—appreciate the same things we would.

We heard a very amusing speaker once who was talking about oxymorons. An oxymoron, he said, is a subject phrase that contains two words that contradict each other and that should mutually exclude each other. He gave some examples:

freezer burn

jumbo shrimp

airline food

military intelligence

postal service

There is another oxymoron of a slightly different type, which people use often and usually with good and pure intent. It is when we say "I *know* how you feel" or "I *see* how you must feel." The reason these are oxymorons is that you can't truly identify with a feeling by seeing it or by knowing it. You can only understand it by feeling it. True empathy, accurately expressed, would therefore have to be "I *feel* how you feel."

I (Richard) was coaching a "biddy basketball team" of kids, ages five to seven, which included two of our boys. A new boy joined the team just before one of the games. His parents dropped him off and left him with us. As a crowd of spectators assembled and the gym became noisy, the new boy started to cry and to say that he didn't want to play. I did all I could to encourage him, but he was so afraid that the best I could do was to get him to quiet down and sit on the bench and watch—with the assurance that he wouldn't have to play unless he wanted to.

A little later I noticed my five-year-old, who had been taken out of the game, sitting with and talking to the new boy. I angled myself closer on the bench so that I could hear. Our boy was saying, "I felt a little scared the first time, too, because there's so many people, but I got used to it, and now it's fun. Don't worry, you'll get used to it too."

So even small children can feel and express concern when the time and situation are just right (and particularly when they have recently been in the same situation themselves). With effort and encouragement older children can go a step beyond this. They can learn to observe, listen to, and feel what others are feeling even when it is not something that has ever happened to them. But it is not easy and it does not happen overnight.

Approaches for Parents

1. Desire. The first "method" for knowing how others feel is to *want* to know how they feel. Most often we do not know because we don't want to. This is not to say that we want *not* to know; we simply don't want to enough to try hard enough to know.

I (Richard) had an employee once who was unhappy in her work and looked as though she might quit. I spent some time with her, talked things over with her, and tried to make her feel better about her job. I was, or so I supposed, exercising some concern by dealing with her feelings.

As I thought back about the experience later that evening, I realized that what I had been doing was not concern for her at all. Actually my concern was for myself. I had realized that if this person quit, my own life would become more difficult. I would have to train another person; it would be inconvenient and time-consuming.

There is nothing inherently wrong with being concerned about your own inconvenience. But do not confuse it with concern for others. And do not expect it to give you any real insight at all into what others are feeling.

Thus we are presented with a classic dilemma and question: If you can't feel with others until you really care about them, how do you develop that caring, which itself is a feeling?

The answer, simple as it sounds, is to *want to*. Want to care! If we start with a desire to care, that desire alone will be enough to make us try to feel what others feel.

2. *Mental effort.* It is the effort we make mentally that gets our thoughts close enough to another person's thoughts that we feel genuine concern. Through hard thought we are capable of getting inside the feelings of someone else.

Our minds actually do have the power to "see" through the eyes and through the feelings of others, but it takes hard mental work. Form the habit of asking yourself as you talk to another person, *What is he feeling right now?* Asking yourself will allow you to see and think in a different way—in a potentially wonderful way.

3. *Applying this mental effort to your children.* Theoretically it should be our children who are the easiest to feel concern for. We do love them enough that their pain is very literally our pain. And they are enough like us that it should be easy for us to re-create in our minds the thoughts and feelings that are in theirs. But it is not easy, simply because of the mental effort it takes. We can get good at it, however, if we put forth the effort and practice.

It's worth it! Once we begin to see through our children's eyes, a whole new world of understanding (and of potential to communicate) opens up to us!

We need to learn to think back. We need to ask ourselves, *How did I feel when I was in fourth grade? What experiences did I have that were similar to these? How did the world look to me at that time? What worried me?*

After we go as far as our memory will take us, we have to go still farther by climbing into the child's shoes and imagining her own vision. *How does this look to her? What is she thinking?*

Effort in this kind of thought can pay great dividends. We knew one father who was terribly upset at the argumentative, rebellious attitude of his son. The boy was not doing anything seriously wrong. He was just disagreeing with his father on everything, arguing just to be contrary, putting forth counterpositions about everything, even when they were silly and illogical.

The father decided one day simply to sit down by himself in a quiet room and try to think what his son was thinking and feel what he was feeling. After less than an hour the father developed a powerful new insight. He realized that the adolescent boy was struggling very hard to feel independent, to begin to become "his own man." To do this, the boy felt that he first had to separate himself a little from his dad, to disagree with him on some things, to have his own position, to have "space" of his own to become his own person. This made him say some things that hurt the father and gave the father sad feelings of not being respected or needed.

Nonetheless, once the father really began to think from the boy's perspective, he realized how natural it is to need to break away from one thing before you can become something on your own. The father realized that he *wanted* his son to be his own man and that an independent opinion now and again was an indispensable part of that process.

The point is that many of the problems of our children are not really their problems but ours. We need to learn to feel their concerns with them before we can really expect them to show genuine concern for us and for others.

4. One-on-one time with a child. A mother recently changed my (Linda's) opinion about my dreams of a chauffeur to take the kids to and from music lessons, dance classes, and basketball practice. "Oh, I wouldn't give up that drive time for anything," she said. "We turn the radio to classical music and talk about feelings." When she said that, I suddenly realized that one of my "trials" could become one of my greatest blessings! The time I was complaining about not having was really there if *I* just set the stage and used it as a time for feelings to be expressed.

5. The argument-ending technique. Remember and use the technique of repeating the other person's position first as discussed in Month 2. For review: A couple sets up a rule of communication that says, "In a disagreement we speak in *turn*, and one person must not make the next point until he or she has repeated or paraphrased the other person's last point to the satisfaction of that other person."

This method promotes a kind of communication and concern, even if it starts as a kind of grudging concern intended to cool tempers and bring people back together.

6. *Delaying "advice" until after "concern."* Often our children complain about something or engage in some behavior we disapprove of, and we rush to advise them, to set them straight, to correct the situation. Our twelve-year-old daughter recently was bemoaning the feeling that no one really liked her, that she had no real friends, and that she felt left out of many of the groups at school. My (Linda's) first impulse was to argue the point with her, to tell her that of course she had friends, that I saw her with them all the time. My next impulse was to counsel her, to tell her she had to quit thinking so much of herself and to "be a friend if she wanted to have friends." Instead, luckily, I just listened and then sat back and told her of a very clearly remembered day when I was twelve, walking home from school by myself, excluded by three boys who seemed to be shunning me. I told her all I could remember of my own similar feelings at her age.

She was suddenly interested and curious. I never did give any advice or solutions that day, but she felt much better, and *we* felt much closer.

Another day our seven-year-old son, Jonah, told me how worried he was about a bully in his class who pushed him every time he walked by and told him he was dumb. I tried to curb my instincts to "solve" and to "interfere." I told my son about a boy named Melvin who used to terrorize me in grade school, who told me he was going to beat me up, who took my homework away every chance he got. I told my son that there came a time the next fall when we started school when I had suddenly grown bigger than Melvin, and he walked up to me, started to say something mean, noticed that I had grown, and just mumbled a quiet "Hi."

Jonah thought that was funny. It made him feel that he could live with his "Melvin." In the days that followed, I would ask him, "How's your Melvin, Jonah?" and we would smile at each other.

Often it is a mistake to think that we can solve our children's problems for them. What we can do is understand them, support them, and give them the subtle encouragements that increase their ability to solve their own problems.

7. Your own methods. List any other ways you can think of to make yourself more interested in the feelings of those you deal with—and more capable of knowing how they feel:

Exercises to Teach Children

1. First-Sunday discussion. Here you come together to establish the family goal for the next month of trying to know the feelings of the other people you deal with. Hold a short discussion with family members ages eight and older, or adapt this to your younger children.

• Read and discuss the Rutledge and Teichner quotes that open this chapter. What do they mean? Why are the ideas important?

The Sunday when we discussed the Rutledge quote in our family happened to be the week after Josh had received his first scouting merit badge. He was obviously proud of himself, and his younger brothers looked at the cloth badge and rubbed it with their fingers as if it were a war medal.

Our eight-year-old thought we ought to have a cheer for Josh similar to one she had learned in school, something like "Yahooo, we're proud of you." It was the beginning of something that has evolved into our family cheer:

Eyre-fire, Eyre-fire
What did you do?
Eyre-fire, Eyre-fire
We're proud of you!

Silly as it is, the kids love it, and it seems to come up whenever someone accomplishes something. It helps remind us not only of the pride we feel in each other but of how much fun it can be to feel happy for others.

At the end of this particular discussion, our fourteen-year-old, proving that she had caught the essence, said that she thought what Rutledge was describing was the *opposite* of jealousy.

- Discuss the story about the five-year-old on the basketball team (page 120). Is it possible to feel what others feel? How do we do so?
- Discuss why it is desirable to feel what another person is feeling. (It gives us chances to help him or her. Also, feeling the feelings of others can give us the opportunity to expand who we are and what we know).
- Discuss what the keys are to knowing how another person feels. (Wanting to know, thinking hard about him or her, and watching and listening.)

2. Prequiz. As usual, begin the month with a short quiz. Save the right-hand columns of everyone's paper so that all can retake the test at the end of the month.

- Make a list of anyone you spent time with last month, and next to his name write down any feelings you think he was experiencing while you were with him.
- About how many times during the month just passed did you ask someone, "How do you feel?"
- How many times during the past month did you give a thoughtful compliment to another person?

3. Giving extra doses of praise. This is intended to reinforce your children's own thoughtfulness.

The objective of this book is to help children worry less about themselves by worrying more about others, but the process involved is a bit of a chicken-and-egg situation. Before children can become very interested in the feelings of others, they need to have a certain base level of self-esteem and confidence in themselves. Children do think less about self as we help them to notice and feel for others, but it is often impossible to raise their awareness of others until their own self-image is strong enough to allow it.

So, all along the way, through every month of this book, we must seek ways to build and nurture our children's self-image. The most direct way to do so is to praise them. Find as many specific little things as you can every day to praise them for. And to the verbal praise add physical touch. A hug, a pat on the back, an arm around the shoulder. This touching reinforces and helps give children the sense of inner well-being that allows them to notice and care how other people are feeling.

Bedtime is a particularly good time to praise a child and reinforce his or her self-image. Compliments at bedtime cause children to go to sleep feeling happy and lend a security and feeling of well-being that often carries over into a child's dreams. Try to find time this month to think of specific compliments to give your children as you tuck them into bed.

4. "The bench" argument resolving technique. This technique teaches children to recognize their own contribution to a fight or disagreement and to appreciate how what they have said could hurt someone else. Whenever two children in your family (of whatever age) are fighting or arguing in an uncontrolled and unpleasant way, try sitting them down together on a bench or side by side on two hard chairs. Tell them that it "takes two to tangle," that they were both at fault in the argument, and that neither one can leave the bench until each has told what *he* or *she* did wrong (not what the other person did wrong).

We have a five-year-old who often ends up "on the bench" but who *never* knows what he did wrong. He hates to sit there, however, so he always asks the child with whom he was fighting what it was that he did wrong. The other child tells him, he repeats it to us, and gets off the bench!

5. The "family tradition" of asking (and answering) "How do you feel?" This will help children become more continuously aware of how other family members feel. Assuming that you have spent the previous month working on congruence ("How Do *I* Feel?"), family members will be at a peak in terms of being able to verbalize how they feel when other family members ask. This month your emphasis should shift from knowing how you yourself feel to wanting to know how other family members feel.

Set the example by simply asking the question often and being genuinely interested in the answer and in what you can do to help whenever the feelings you listen to are sad or negative.

Asking other family members how they feel may seem like something too obvious and simple to mention, but it is, against the backdrop of last month's work on knowing and expressing our own feelings, the most effective and useful place to start.

6. Role-reversal games. This activity can give another perspective to parent-child views of one another. Children often enjoy assuming the role of parent for an evening, particularly if parents play the role of children. If you really get into it, both sides can learn a lot. Let them, as kids playing the role of parents, ask whether you've done your homework, push you to clean your room, and try to get you to go to bed on time. Respond to them with the emotions that their demands cause you to feel. Try *hard* to project yourself into what their feelings would be, and encourage them to do the same with yours.

After you have tried this role-playing for an evening or two, try to use the skills and ideas of it in day-to-day life, and encourage your children to do likewise. For example the next time your son is out too late, try projecting yourself into how he might feel (maybe he's having too much fun to remember the time; maybe he's concerned that he's not home but the other kids he's with are persuading him to stay out). Hopefully your son will be trying to project also. (*How are my parents feeling—worried about me, trusting me but wishing I'd call if I can't be home on time?*)

7. *More specific and specialized forms of question and answer.* This will help children discover the enjoyment of finding out interesting things about others. By example, by encouragement, and through frequent family discussion, train your children to find out all they tactfully can about other people—where they come from, what they like to do, what they're interested in, what their plans are, who else they know, and so forth.

Again, example is the most impressive teacher. We can think back to a time when we had taken two of our children out to eat and happened to sit at a table next to a very interesting English couple. We asked them a couple of questions and quickly became engaged in a most intriguing and far-ranging discussion. Our children didn't say much, but they listened.

After the experience each of the children who had been with us expressed feelings of empathy for the English couple—and very real interest in them. Our nine-year-old said, "Dad, those people were interesting! When we first started talking to them, I thought they were really *different*, but the more we talked, the more I thought they were a lot like us!" She paused for a moment and then went on, "You sure thought of a lot of good questions to ask them, Dad!"

It's fun, around the dinner table or whenever there is a moment to talk, to ask, "Who found someone interesting to ask questions of today?" Get the children interested not only in asking questions but in telling the rest of the family what they have learned.

8. *Visiting old people, people from other cultures, and so on.* This activity is designed to give children opportunities to empathize with people who are very different from themselves. When children are only around their peers, it is easy for them to assume that others think pretty much the same way and have the same emotions as they do. On the other hand, when they are exposed to very different people, their ability to empathize has many opportunities to expand and stretch itself.

Our own family has been involved with some young students from Malaysia and with a very elderly man whom we have been trying to help. As the children talk to these people, ask them questions, and try to guess how they are feeling, they begin to see many of the things they have taken for granted from a very different perspective. And they learn new ways to feel by feeling vicariously for the other person.

9. *More responsibility.* A Harvard study found that in cultures where adolescents are given more responsibility, there is more altruism and extracenteredness and less self-centeredness. It is in societies like our own, where too much is given and too little is expected, that teenagers show such propensity to be insensitive to others and

wrapped up in their own needs and wants. We must recognize this connection and realize that one purpose of giving responsibility is to help children get their minds off
themselves.

Like many families we have always had family jobs to
which children were assigned. There was one period, however, when we dropped the jobs. The temporary change
accomplished what we had expected it would—and it also
taught us something we hadn't expected or thought about.

We had begun to worry that the children were doing
their jobs out of assignment and threat rather than out of
any real desire to help. So in a Sunday meeting we announced for the time being they wouldn't have any jobs.
We told them that we had heard too much of "That's not
my job" or "This isn't fair." We would rather do everything ourselves than hear the complaining, we said, so we
had decided just to do everything ourselves for a week. We
did so, and then the following week we invited the children to help out if they really wanted to. We tried never to
demand or insist. We just asked, "Would you *like* to do
. . ." and quickly added, "If you don't that's okay. I'll be
glad to do it."

As it turned out, they did their jobs better than they
ever had before and ended up saying in the next Sunday
meeting that they did want their jobs and would try to do
them without complaining. The other thing we noticed,
which bore out the study mentioned earlier, is that the
children were particularly self-centered and more withdrawn from us and from each other during the week when
they didn't have jobs.

Nothing is more gratifying to a parent than seeing a
child accept responsibility and handle a challenge with
maturity and sensitivity. Our oldest daughter, Saren, loves

drama. She has always begged to be taken to auditions for plays. Sometimes she won the audition, which in turn required hundreds of trips to the rehearsal hall for practices and performances. The summer she turned sixteen, we decided to let her try her hand at directing a play—*Annie*—in the small farm town of Dingle, Idaho. We were spending our summer there and had a built-in "Annie"—our ten-year-old daughter, Saydi, who had been singing "Tomorrow" to any audience she could find for seven years.

We totally turned the project over to Saren (with great trepidation). To our amazement she grabbed the baton and ran. All summer she worked. First she had auditions, talked her sister Shawni into taking a part, and tried to talk her dad *out* of taking one. She succeeded with the sister but failed with the dad. He said he was born to play President Roosevelt.

Richard and I rubbed our hands with glee all summer as this very shy but strong-willed, often self-centered sixteen-year-old daughter of ours blossomed into a capable, sensitive director. She was concerned about creating a place for a few "street urchins" who hadn't made it when they auditioned as "orphans." She knew how they felt! She empathized!

She was patient and sensitive with everyone—even her sometimes temperamental sisters and bossy father. Her strong will was her "best suit" as she tactfully but firmly let everyone know that it must be done *her* way. Even the dog, Sandy, followed her directions! Besides being the director, she was the choreographer and set designer. Of my hundred thousand suggestions she kindly accepted about two. I learned early to stay out of it and let her do things her own way.

On opening night I really expected sort of a junior high production. But with the help of many wonderful actors and assistants, that young lady pulled off a very professional play, one of the best I've ever seen. (Of course I may be a little prejudiced.) They played to a sellout crowd for three nights, and the proceeds were donated to the local church. I was astounded! Even more than that, I was thrilled at the growing sensitivity of this very interesting person living in our home.

10. *Game: Listen, paraphrase, and add feelings.* This game is intended to improve children's listening and interpretation skills. Explain to them that the listening ability your family worked on in Month 2 is just the start for being able to understand other people's feelings. You have to listen, to understand, and then to try hard to put yourself into other people's shoes and to imagine what they feel.

The game goes as follows: One family member asks another what happened to him or her that day. The second person tells some experience, and the first person repeats back or paraphrases the experience, visualizing it as though it had happened to him. He then indicates how he thinks the other person felt.

Example: Twelve-year-old James says to ten-year-old Pat, "What happened today?" Pat says, "Oh, we had a math test and I thought it would be easy, but the teacher asked a lot of questions from the chapter I didn't study and hardly any from the chapter I did!"

James says, "So you thought you were prepared for the test, because you did study, but you mostly studied one chapter and when you took the test, most of it was on another chapter—one that you hadn't studied. I'll bet you felt kind of frustrated, and maybe you felt a little bit mad at your teacher for tricking you or for not telling you what chapter to study."

It's surprising how much children *enjoy* this kind of discussion with their siblings or with their parents, once they get the hang of it. And there is no better training for the development of real concern.

11. *Your own ideas.* Take the time to think of other ways you could help your children become more aware of the feelings of the people around them, and list your ideas here:

12. *Postquiz.* On the "first Sunday" of the next month retake the test you started this month with to review and reinforce what has been learned. As usual, review everyone's answers and discuss how far you have all come in wanting to know others' feelings, and in asking and finding out what others are feeling.

When we took this postquiz, we became aware of the amazing capacity that adolescents have for noticing and interpreting the feelings of other people once they put their minds to it. Our ten-year-old told of a man she had observed during a family trip we had taken on a tourist boat. She said he looked lonely and "uncomfortable." He "looked like a grandpa," she said, but he didn't have anyone with him and maybe he was wondering if he should have come to such a fun place all by himself. She said that whenever the boat went around a corner and the man saw something, he looked like he wanted to show it to someone else.

Family Focal Point—Collecting Friends

During this fourth month we put up a big chart by the dinner table called the Friends Chart. On it there is a column for each member of our family where we can write the name of each new person we meet and find out about. There is a bit of competition about who can get the most new friends on the chart each month, but the rule is that no name can be listed unless we have *found out something about that person that helps us know how he or she feels.*

Example: Seven-year-old Jonah listed a new friend he had met and told us that this boy "really liked school but hated to go home afterward because he didn't have any brothers or sisters and he felt lonely."

Just having the list in a visible place and discussing an entry once in a while is enough to keep children aware of the goal of getting to know people and discovering their feelings.

At the end of the year when we're doing greeting cards (in our case it's Thanksgiving cards rather than Christmas cards), we go through the Friends Chart and make sure each one gets a card.

Summary

Deep within us is the potential to see and hear everything and to feel every level of every emotion. We are stopped from fully seeing, from fully feeling, by the filters and blockades and blind spots that our egos and self-centeredness put in front of us—by our windows turning into mirrors.

The goal is to become transparent, to become less and less aware of ourselves and of our problems as we become more aware of everything around us. As we ask ourselves more often, "How does this person feel?" we will have less and less time to ask ourselves (or to worry about) how *we* feel.

And once we gain a little ability in knowing the feelings of those we talk to and deal with, we can move to a higher form of concern, one in which we try to become aware of the feelings of people we are not in direct contact or conversation with. Such is the focus of the next month.

Empathy:

"How Does the Other Person Feel"

See how the masses of men worry themselves into nameless graves while here and there a great unselfish soul forgets himself into immortality.

—RALPH WALDO EMERSON

Help me to understand, Oh Lord, that understanding others is the key to being understood.

—SAINT FRANCIS OF ASISSI

Illustrations and Stories

Answering the question "How do you feel?" with regard to another person with whom you are dealing or interacting is essentially a matter of concern. Through observing, through asking and listening, and through caring, we remove our attention from ourselves and focus it in the form of *concern* on the person with whom we are dealing.

A somewhat more difficult form of the same skill involves asking, "How does *he* or *she* feel? referring to someone we are *not* interacting with, someone who is not telling us how he or she feels, someone whose only connection with us is the empathy we feel for that person.

"I had a good time in school today, " said Jonah, our nine-year-old fourth-grader. "There was a new boy from Australia in our class. The other kids kind of laughed at his accent. I made a friend of him. He is really a nice guy. Can I invite him to play?"

"Were you remembering how you felt when we moved last?" I asked.

"Yeah, I think so," he said, smiling. "The first few weeks were not much fun," he added with a roll of the eyes.

The Latin roots of the word *empathy* mean "to feel with." Because Jonah had "been there," he was able actually to "feel with" that new boy. Although it was a difficult thing for him at the time, our move and the struggle to fit in had taught him an invaluable lesson in empathy.

We sometimes forget, as parents, how cruel children can be to one another. We forget until something reminds us, and then we realize how important it is to teach our children to ask themselves often, *How does the other person feel?*

We were reminded rather forcefully of the need one Sunday when we heard a thirteen-year-old girl speak in church. What she said made such an impression that we had her write it out for us.

When I was in the third grade, I'd just moved here and I became friends with a girl named Sharon. We were best friends and inseparable at school. By the time we were in the fourth grade we had another friend, Carrie. Carrie, Sharon, and I were the very best of friends. We even called ourselves the Three Musketeers! We were great friends for two or three months, and then it seemed that only Sharon and I were friends, or Carrie and Sharon, or Carrie and I. Finally it ended with Carrie and Sharon. They would tease me day in and day out. They called me up just to tell me how ugly or how stupid I was. At recess they would call me names and tell me I was dumb, or fat, or ugly. They would constantly tell me that I wasn't capable of anything, and I *believed them!* The last day of school they called me up and said, "I'm so glad that school's out because now we don't have to look at ugly people like you."

In fifth grade I was in a different room than they, for obvious reasons. Every time I saw them, I hated them for what they had done to me. Eventually I forgave them and I learned a real valuable lesson from this experience: I learned to *always* listen to your friends, and *never* put them down; *always* be there when they need you; and *always* care no matter what. When I do these things, I have a better relationship with my friends and I feel better about myself. These two girls taught me to care about people and their feelings.

My mother has always told me that to have a friend, you must be a friend.

In every elementary school, in every class, there is a class "reject." Well, our class reject was Dora. I was always friends with Dora, and as a result people thought I was a reject too. In seminary in ninth grade we had a thing on Valentine's Day where we could write a note to someone else in another class. Well, Dora wrote one to me and it said, "Dear Dawn, Thank you for being my only friend." I was so grateful that I had been her friend even though people thought I was dumb too."

We once saw a movie called *Brainstorm*, which contained an interesting central idea that a machine could be hooked up to two people and allow one to see, hear, and feel everything that the other person was feeling, as though he or she was actually in the mind and body of the other person.

The movie was science fiction. But in real life there *is* a device that allows us to transform our own perceptions and feelings into those of another person. The device is not a machine; it is an almost magical quality and skill called *empathy*.

Assuming that others see things the same way we do is as silly as assuming that our eyeglasses would work for everyone else. The Golden Rule is a marvelous code of conduct and, with slight variations in wording, has a place in virtually every major philosophy and theology in the world. Because of the differences in people, however, the law reaches its highest and most beautiful level *not* with the words "Do unto others as you would have them do unto you" but "Do unto others as *they* would wish to be done unto."

Our daughter Shawni at age eight had gone along on her brother Josh's sixth birthday party to "help out." It was a snow-sledding party in January, and there were about a dozen six-year-old boys.

I (Richard) had become occupied with getting the hot chocolate ready and was standing with Josh when Shawni came up, tapped Josh on the shoulder, and in a very concerned voice pointed first at one boy and then at another and asked Josh their names. Then she said, "Well, Billy doesn't look very happy. Two of the other boys wouldn't let him go on their tube and I think he is about to cry. And John looks a little scared. He still hasn't gone down the hill. You should go talk to them, Josh, and make them both feel happy—because you don't want anyone to be sad at your party."

Shawni said all this with the utmost concern, and Josh took her suggestion very seriously. He went right over and talked to John, then got a big tube and went down the hill with him and Billy.

The day and the experience are clear and vivid in our memory because of the simple, sure example it provided of young children's ability to be highly empathetic.

Crabs have an interesting instinct to pull each other back. When catching crabs on the beach, you don't need a high-sided bucket to put them in. A shallow pan will do— as long as you have at least two crabs in it. If one tries to climb out, the other will instinctively reach up and pull him back. People, especially children, often behave much like crabs. If someone gets ahead of us, outachieves us, or seems more popular, our instinct is to pull him down in some way—perhaps by gossip or by rationalizing that whatever he has done is not that important.

It is our nature to think of others as various kinds of mirrors for our own reflection. Around people of whom we are jealous we tend to see ourselves reflected back as being inadequate, so we often try to stop looking at them or to "pull them down," at least in our own minds.

The ability to shift into "windows" and to see people for what they are, what their feelings and needs are—and to take pleasure in their accomplishments as we would in our own—involves the most profound change of perspective that a person can undergo.

The opposite of empathy is envy or jealousy. And it is so much easier to notice what someone else *has* (that we want) than to notice what they *need* (that we could give).

Approaches for Parents

1. Visualize. The skill called visualization has great application this month as we try to understand how others feel. In various cultures, for widely varying purposes and through widely varied techniques, human beings have proven their ability and potential to visualize or to imagine something in a way that makes it as real as if it *were* real.

In the myth of Camelot, Merlin the magician taught young Arthur to see all perspectives by *becoming* the eagle or the stag, or even the tree, in order to feel what they feel, see what they see, grasp what they grasp.

In the highest form of martial arts—the levels above the black belt—the ninja masters learn to sense and visualize things their eyes cannot see, to feel and anticipate the energy of movement, even that which is occurring behind them, and to defend against it even before it is enacted.

Many current popular writers tell us how to visualize our illnesses as cured and our bodies as healed, and the results are often both tangible and remarkable. The advocates of self-improvement, from meditation experts to positive-mental-attitude speakers, tell us that *thoughts* can become specific and focused enough to control *things*.

Besides learning to listen, we need to learn how to visualize. Listening helps us be sensitive to how things really are. Visualizing how they *can* be is what allows us to change things for the better—for ourselves and for others.

A great chef once told us that he believed all truly good cooks had the ability to read a recipe carefully and, without so much as touching or mixing a single ingredient, taste the outcome.

Great composers hear music while reading notes on a printed page.

Poets feel the wind they are describing with their pen.

Artists see their picture in their mind's eye long before they put paint to canvas.

Good baseball pitchers see the path the ball will take before they release it from their hand.

And parents—those who observe their children and listen to them—begin to visualize the people they can grow to become long before the years pass that lead to their vision.

The gift and skill of visualization is at the heart of our potential ability to feel as others feel. We have the power to observe something or somebody closely from the outside and then to project ourselves into that thing or person to experience that existence from the inside.

Practice this and see how quickly you can master it. Observe a tree intently. Look at it from bottom to top, studying its trunk, its bark, its limbs, its leaves, and so on. Then imagine yourself as the tree—inside the tree looking out. See the landscape around you, feel the wind blowing your leaves, feel the sap flowing inside of you. Try this with objects and with people. It is a learned skill that takes practice. But as you become capable of it, your capacity for sensitivity will grow dramatically. And once you are good at visualizing things and feelings as they *are* you can begin to visualize them as they *could be*.

2. *Turn the eye into a camera shutter.* It is people's faces, particularly their eyes, that give us our best clues to their feelings and their needs.

And our own eyes, when trained to do so, can read a face in an instantaneous glance. One way to train the eye (a fun and interesting way) is to walk along a busy street and take "eye snapshots" of each person you pass.

Look at the face intently and then blink, fixing the face in your mind as a still shot, as though you had just pressed the shutter of your camera. Let your mind interpret and analyze the face you just took a snapshot of. What did you see? What was in the eyes? The lines of the face? The tilt of the head? Think about the image.

Our own minds surprise us when we really turn them loose and simply let them imagine what each person might be thinking.

On a crowded street your eyes may take a snapshot every couple of seconds, so your first impression of a face will be your only impression. Just look at a face, blink, and let your mind give you the quickest interpretation it can make: "worried," "excited," "intense," "confused," "lost in thought."

As with the development of any skill, practice will make you better. Somewhat like a muscle, the mind's interpretive powers strengthen with use. Before long you will find that one quick glance can give you very strong impressions about what another person is feeling. And you will feel quite sure that your impression is correct. It is almost as though your mind has the power to make quick contact with another mind through some sort of eye contact or wave transmission that we do not consciously understand.

This kind of snapshot thinking is hard mental work, but it is the best and simplest form of empathy training we know.

3. Be an "optometrist." The reason people see well with their glasses is that the optometrist started with that person's perspective and vision, not with his or her own. It is much more difficult to do this in regular life. We rarely start with what the other person sees. Rather we insist that he or she should see the way we do.

During this month try to be an optometrist. Try to be interested enough in other people that you actually start with what you imagine they see.

4. *Practice putting your desire to understand above your other desires.* Picture in your mind a father who is upset at his son for not finishing some tasks he was assigned to do after school. The boy wants to explain. The father is interested in why the boy didn't do anything, but he is more interested in shaping the boy up. Therefore he doesn't really listen.

So often we don't really listen because we have other desires that are much stronger than our desire to understand. This month make a conscious effort to put your desire to understand above any other wants. It will make a remarkable difference in how much you understand and empathize with other people, particularly with your children.

5. *Your own methods.* List any other ideas that come to you on how to better ask and better answer the question "How does he (or she) feel?"

Exercises to Teach Children

1. First-Sunday discussion. This activity is intended to shift family focus for the coming month to the goal of becoming able to sense how others are feeling, even when we are not with them or talking to them. As usual, begin this new month with a discussion among all family members age eight or older, and adapt this for smaller children.

- Discuss what it would be like to have a machine like the one in the movie *Brainstorm* (see Illustrations and Stories section).
- Tell the stories of "Linda at the dance" (Month 2) and "Shawni at Josh's birthday party" (this month) and discuss what happens when we watch for how others are feeling.
- Remind everyone that we worked last month on knowing how the person you were talking to was feeling. This month we will be trying to know how people feel without asking them or even talking to them. Will this be harder? Is it even possible?
- What are the ways we can know how another person feels? One way is to experience exactly what others are experiencing, to "walk in their moccasins." Another way is to think hard about them and to use our minds and our imaginations to know how they feel.

2. Prequiz. (Remember to save everyone's paper for the requiz the next "first Sunday.")

- List as many people as you can whom you noticed lately (but didn't talk to) and write down how you thought they might be feeling.
- Describe the most interesting face you can remember seeing during the month just passed. What was interesting about the face? What feelings might have made the face look like it did?
- Whom have you noticed lately who needed help? What kind of help did he or she need?

3. Provide an example. As always, this is the best method of all. Simply make yourself more aware of others, and talk about your awareness of others, especially in the presence of your children. Notice the looks on people's faces and comment on them. Watch things such as the posture and mannerisms of people as well as their circumstances and situations.

I (Linda) observed a mother one day in London who was marvelous at this. She was sitting on the upper level of a red bus with her daughter, who looked to be ten or eleven years old. As the bus picked its way through the crowded city streets, the mother, in a voice that had more interest in it than authority, was saying things like, "Look at that older man, at his face. He looks awfully worried about something," or "Those two girls look like they're having a good time. What would you guess they're talking about, just by watching them?"

4. Look for motives rather than blame. This activity is intended to help children shift their own negative feelings to the more positive mental energy of trying to understand others. When your child tells you of having been hurt or offended by another child, resist the temptation to overprotect or to become angry or vindictive toward the other child or the other child's parents.

Instead sit down with your child and together try to figure out why the other child might have said or did what he or she did. Say, "What might have made him angry enough or jealous enough or upset enough to do that?" If no reason is obvious, speculate on what it might have been. (Maybe his father was mad at him today. Maybe he felt left out in some social situation. Maybe he flunked a test.)

Whether you discover the true motive or not, you will succeed in turning your child's attention from his or her own problem to the possible problem of someone else.

5. *Game: Put yourself in the picture.* This game lets children practice empathizing with people they have never met or spoken to. Watch for pictures in magazines that show people in situations that are unusual to you and your children. These could range from a man on a horse in the mountains to a girl in a magazine clothing ad. Almost any magazine has several pictures or advertisements that will work for this exercise.

The game consist of looking at the picture and attempting to describe how the person in the picture *feels*. This can start on a physical level as you try to imagine what he sees and hears, whether she is cold or warm, and so forth. Then try to go beyond the physical and speculate how he or she might feel emotionally. Have a discussion about it. Let each person imagine how the subject feels and express his or her own observations.

A variation of the game for older children is to give each player a different picture to study, then have them give a short speech or write a brief theme on what the subject feels.

6. *Lavish praise.* The purpose of this is to reinforce

and bolster even the smallest evidences of empathy so that it is more likely to occur again. One of our daughters came to the dinner table one night with tears in her eyes. We asked what was wrong and she tried to shrug it off and say she was okay. When we persisted, she broke down a bit and said she had been looking in a magazine at pictures of starving children in Ethiopia. She fought back the tears of her very genuine concern and quietly added that she wanted to send a hundred dollars (most of her bank account) to help out.

Her whole attitude was so beautiful that we found ourselves praising her for days—not always in open, verbal ways, but with a look, an arm around her shoulder, a glance of pride, and an added desire to be with her and do things with her.

Thinking back, we realize that our natural reaction to Shawni during that week did more to motivate her brothers and sisters toward similar efforts at empathy than any method or technique we had ever tried.

Watch for extracentered actions. Listen for comments that indicate efforts to understand others and their situations. And praise these insights and actions with lavish and specific compliments.

While munching an after-school snack one day, eleven-year-old Saydi said, "Mom, there's this girl in our class at school that everyone makes fun of. She doesn't have very nice clothes and she talks kind of funny. Today the kids were making fun of her. I was standing with three of my friends at one of our science stations and they started talking and giggling about her funny socks. I didn't quite know what to do, so I just walked away. Then at recess I decided to go over and talk to her. She was all alone and I knew that if I went, the other kids would think that I was dumb, too, but I just thought about it and decided to go anyway. I just got to know her. She's really nice."

Saydi is not one of our children who is at a loss for words. Sometimes it takes me fifteen minutes to get a word in edgewise. She always tells me everything I've ever wanted to know and more! But when she finally finished, I (Linda) think I praised her for at least three minutes. We repeated her experience at dinner and asked the other children to watch for similar chances to help. They were quick to point out that it was easier for Saydi than it was for them because she was a natural daredevil and blabbermouth—but they agreed to try!

7. Broaden perspective with travel and experience. This allows children to observe firsthand the different situations that others find themselves in and to appreciate their perspective. We mentioned in Month 4 how much perspective and insight children can gain through travel and exposure to various "other ways." The experiences gleaned from travel can take children a step beyond perspective and can foster empathy.

As interesting as the magazine-perspective game (Exercise 5) can be, real people from different environments are much more instructive and educational. When parents make the effort to make use of the experience, any form of travel can be an "empathy experience" for children. The more the people are different from what children are used to, the more interesting it is to attempt empathy. Simply observe together and ask children the right questions. ("How would that feel, to do what that man does every day?" "What do you think makes that person look so happy?" "What are the main differences in her typical day and yours?")

Some travel is not very expensive—and even at home

many of these same techniques can be employed while watching a TV documentary or in any other setting where you are observing cultures and people who are very different from yourself.

Be careful not to emphasize the negative or to breed criticism or excess pity in your children through this type of observation. Lean in the opposite direction by looking for the good and the positive. Say, "Yes, it is dirtier and the houses are smaller, but what makes that person look like he feels so good?" or "Why do you think these people are so friendly and open?" or "Is our way of doing that really better, or is it just different?"

Our eight-year-old provided a good example of how profound a child's observations can be as we were returning from a trip to Mexico. "What is the most interesting thing you learned?" was our question. Her answer: "I learned you don't need to have shoes to be happy."

You can also have a closer-to-home experience (without travel, new environments, or even TV documentaries). In most every community, large or small, there are people who are potentially interesting to your children because of their different lifestyles and perspectives. Again, the differences are valuable because they stretch and develop the skills of empathy.

As mentioned earlier, we once "adopted" four eighteen-year-old Malaysian students who attend the university near our home. They needed American friends and we decided we needed them to broaden our family's circle of acquaintances. We had them over or took them places with us two or three times a month. Our children had a whole new world opened up to them as they became our friends. They were Muslim and had different traditions, different styles, different goals and plans. Their curiosity in us sparked our children's curiosity in them and gave us endless opportunities to ask our children, "How do you think they feel?"

8. *Miss a meal.* When you miss a meal for a purpose, it can help children to emphasize physically and to become more acquainted with the basic idea of trying to feel others' needs. From age eight, and often earlier, children are capable of fasting for at least one meal. With the kind of discussion and observations that parents can add, this can be one of the most basic and meaningful early empathetic experiences they have. Talk about the feeling of hunger as it is experienced and about how it might feel if it went on for days if they, like nearly one-third of the children in the world, went to bed hungry each night.

This method is particularly instructive if you can use the money you save by missing a meal to help someone who is hungry. Some families sponsor a child in a Third World country through one of the relief organizations; they receive pictures and letters from a real human being, who is being fed by the money they save through fasting.

As children come to understand and appreciate the idea of missing a meal to help someone else, they will feel a certain physical empathy, which can be a good analogy by which to begin feeling the deeper forms of emotional, social, and even spiritual empathy. As you talk about how hunger feels, ask also how they think people feel who have no friends or whose parents don't care about them.

9. *Face read.* This is intended to stimulate children's interest in trying to empathize by sight. Explain to your children that just as it takes some time to learn to read letters and words, it takes time and practice to learn to read faces, but it is possible. Tell them of your own efforts to do this and of any experience you had with the kind of

"camera shutter" eye blinking suggested in this month's "Approaches for Parents."

Encourage them to practice face reading whenever possible. Do it with them. Discuss together how to do it. Simply look hard at a stranger's face. But instead of just noticing features and expressions and the amount of light in the eye, try to look beyond the surface of the face and see the emotions. Look for stress, for love, for insecurity, for confidence, and for every other observable emotion.

10. Interesting-person game. This game can bring about greater interest in the "How does he or she feel?" question by sharing an "interesting face" with other family members. Start a tradition at dinner of occasionally asking, "Tell us about the most interesting person you saw today!" This is an extension of the "interesting thing" game of Month 1. Each person should try to recall his or her face-reading activities of the day and describe to other family members the most interesting person he or she observed that day.

A sample answer from a ten-year-old: "At the bus stop I saw an older lady who had been shopping. She was short and a little stooped over, but she was big and wide and strong enough to carry two big shopping bags. Her face looked pleasant. It had deep smile lines by her mouth and her eyes. She looked at me, and when I smiled, she smiled and said hello. I think she's probably a grandma with some nice grandchildren. I think she likes her life and I don't think she minds being old."

11. Retard children's social growth. This is intended to keep them somewhat out of the "peer-group-selfishness syndrome". We once asked a favorite older couple that we know for further advice on rearing children, and their very interesting response was "Retard their social growth." We have found many useful interpretations for that phrase over the years, but perhaps the most useful one is the desirability of limiting adolescent social schedules in order to allow more time for them to be influenced by their own thoughts and by their parents' example.

Attempt to make popularity a "nongoal" among your children. Point out that those who seek to be liked, to fit in, and to be just like everyone else are thinking too much *about* themselves and not thinking enough *for* themselves.

How early you want your children to involve themselves in various social situations is a very personal thing. In our family children do not date in one-on-one situations until they are sixteen. Major school functions and group dates sometimes qualify as exceptions. Time spent with friends is limited, as are sleepovers. We are more liberal in having other children stay at our home than in letting our children stay elsewhere.

And we try to talk often about how it is better to be respected and liked as an individual than to be popular and how it is better to be yourself than to be like everyone else.

Of course children's friends are an important part of their lives, but too much time with friends can create as many problems for one child as not having enough friends does for another.

Some of our children think they would like to *live* with their friends. (Some days we think that sounds like a good idea too!) Some children are wonderful influences and good friends. Others have a negative effect on our children. In those cases we have had long talks with the child involved to try to encourage him or her to be a leader for the right instead of letting the other person influence the child to do something wrong. In some cases we've had talks with the friend too.

Time with family, time to study and read, time to learn a musical instrument or other skill—all of these can be jeopardized if too much time is spent with friends. And too-early dating is generally pretty awkward and socially uncomfortable as well as dangerous, in the sense that it poses a risk of too much physical involvement.

12. *Your own methods.* List any other ideas you can think of for training children to watch others and empathize with what they may be feeling:

13. *Postquiz.* The next "first Sunday," as you complete this month and start the next, retake the quiz from the beginning of this chapter. Everyone will do much better on it. Discuss your answers and ask if it is important to keep on looking for others' feelings even as your family goes on to the next chapter. Hopefully everyone will say yes, and you can then introduce the family focal point as a way of keeping everybody doing it.

Family Focal Point—"Think-Abouts"

"Think-Abouts" can keep children aware on an ongoing basis of the special needs of other people. *Each Sunday at dinner,* discuss one or more particular *needs* that someone has noticed during the past week. This will involve not only remembering what you have noticed but *thinking* hard about how someone feels and about what you might do for him or her. In our family we usually end up discussing several needs that various family members have noticed or become aware of (from very broad things, such

as peace in a war-torn part of the world, to very narrow and specific things, such as recovery for the older lady next door who had fallen and broken her hip).

The point is that the weekly discussion can become a weekly reminder and motivator to think about How does he or she feel?

Summary

It is impossible to know all of the motives and all of the inner thoughts of any other person. It is not impossible, however, to feel *with* another person empathetically—enough that we know much of how he or she feels. And efforts to do so are the best training for sensitivity that can ever be devised.

The same perspectives and appreciation that can come through reduced circumstances can be had without personal crisis if we are willing to bear one another's burdens and to feel empathy deeply enough to feel as others feel.

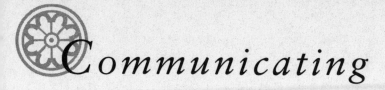

Communicating

Observations, insights, and empathic feelings are of limited use without the ability to communicate them effectively.

The skills of verbalizing and expressing what we see, what we feel, and what we care about in others become the tools that allow us to comfort, to help, to contribute, and to form deep relationships.

UNDERSTANDING

OBSERVING

FEELING

COMMUNICATING

+DOING

=SENSITIVITY

Expressing What We See

Those who learn to express what they see ... see more.

Communication is the thread that ties all people to each other. Remove it and there is no society, no civilization, and perhaps no love.

Illustrations and Stories

During the three years we lived in England we were consistently delighted by the ability of the British to use their own language correctly. Slang is little used in southern England, nor is fuzzy or imprecise speech of any kind. English is spoken clearly and articulately and is used with precision and pride by children as well as by adults, by workers and manual laborers as well as by educated professionals.

I recall standing in the hallway of our children's elementary school (infant school, the British call it) waiting for our children and tuning in on several of the conversations that surrounded me. The children's words were crisp and precise, their sentence structure impeccable. Their questions were insightful and specific. And these were second- and third-graders. It was our first month in England, and my assumption was that all the kids were geniuses. Very soon, as our own children competed well in school, I realized that it was language, not brain power, in which the British kids were superior.

Shortly thereafter we needed a plumber to unstop a drain. The fellow who came (dressed in a black suit and tie), was a delightful conversationalist who spoke with such clarity that I kept him for an hour after he'd fixed the drain, enjoying a conversation that ranged over and across several subjects.

A television editorial captured rather well the overriding importance of communication and language skills. It went as follows:

> One of the charms of the English language is its constant ability to change and evolve. We add new words and new expressions with relative ease, and we eliminate those which have outlived their usefulness.
>
> But illiteracy should never serve as the basis for the evolution of language. For example, the young starlet who insists on peppering her conversation with "you knows" and salting it with "he goes" is not likely to add to the flavor of the language or detract from the blandness of her thoughts.
>
> Neither language nor thought are improved by the radio announcer who consistently mispronounces "consortium" as "consorteeum," or who redundantly reminds listeners it is raining outside. (Where else does it rain?)
>
> These examples seem minor—and perhaps they are—but there is a direct correlation between accuracy of language and accuracy of thought. George Orwell once wrote: "A man may take to drink because he feels himself to be a failure, and then fail all the more completely because he

drinks. It is rather the same thing that is happening to the English language. It becomes ugly and inaccurate because our thoughts are foolish, but the slovenliness of our language makes it easier for us to have foolish thoughts. If thought corrupts language, language can also corrupt thought!" Language is never far removed from thought." Careless language leads to careless thought . . . and vice versa.

In this book we worked first on the skills of seeing, listening, and feeling. Now we attempt to add the ability of communicating all of those things to other people.

It is well to remember, however, that the learning doesn't always happen in this order. The ability to communicate, the striving to gain that ability, and the practicing of that ability can cause us to observe more, to listen better, and to feel more deeply.

Our oldest daughter, partially because her earliest schooling was in England, is exceptionally articulate. As she entered the stormy beginning of her adolescence, she was hit with her share of problems. They ranged from shyness to moodiness to various kinds of rebellion against authority. So many times our ability to help her with her difficulties hinged on her ability to conceptualize her thoughts and communicate them to us. She had (and has) a certain pride in her ability to verbalize things, and it has often been that pride and our confidence in her logical and articulate communication abilities that have prompted her to express her feelings, clarify them in her own mind, and give us the opportunity to help.

It is a basic fact of life that we can't do much about who we are or how we feel until we can describe and communicate it.

This month is devoted to the pursuit of the ability to communicate what we *observe*—what we see, hear, and otherwise receive through our physical senses. The ability to communicate these things is a prerequisite for Month 7, which focuses on the skill of communicating feelings.

Approaches for Parents

1. Careful speech. Most of us are capable of speaking much better than we do. Conscious effort to say more precisely what we mean is the best practice for becoming more articulate.

A by-product of more careful speech is that we don't speak so hastily. Once a person forms the mental habit of thinking for an instant or two before talking, two major benefits come about: He avoids saying things he shouldn't say, and he says more clearly and expresses more exactly what he wishes to communicate.

By "careful speech" we do not mean the use of more big words or more complex sentences. In fact the opposite is often true. The best communicators (writers as well as speakers) usually use direct, simple language. But their words are well thought out and carefully chosen.

A commitment to communicate more clearly will lead to: (a) more independent thought; (b) a broader vocabulary; (c) more honest and stimulating conversation; (d) less slang and less meaningless generalities in language; and (e) children who follow your example in being clear and precise.

2. Take time to write (whether you're good at it or not). It's only recently that we have begun telling people just how the books in this "Teaching Children" series came to be written. They were not originally intended for publication. We wrote *Teaching Your Children Joy . . . Responsibility,* and . . . *Values* for ourselves because we needed a philosophy for raising our own children, and we felt that writing was the best way to clarify and complete our thoughts.

Writing has a way of clarifying and organizing people's minds, of taking random thoughts and ideas and putting them together in ways that make sense.

During this month we challenge you as parents once again to devote a few minutes each day to writing. We made a similar challenge back in Month 1. The focus then was on observing. Here the focus is on communicating more clearly and precisely about the things we observe. As you accept this challenge, you will put yourself in a position to get your children to be doing more writing, as suggested in the next part of this chapter. Try writing at least two or three times a week in one or more of the following ways:

- *Journal.* Record your observations at the end of each day. Concentrate as much on the thoughts you have had as on the events that have transpired.
- *Poetry.* Write a short poem about one thing that happens each day or about one observation you make.
- *Letters.* Write descriptive and informative letters to loved ones. Don't rely on phone calls to stay in touch. It's so much better to end up with a stack of expressive letters than a stack of expensive phone bills. Strive to be precise and clear, both about events you are describing and about thoughts you wish to express. This is especially fun for parents

who want to describe the weekly adventures of their household. For years when we lived away from our families, Linda's weekly letters home were our best record and most complete journal.

3. Further develop the Rogerian technique of listening discussed in Month 2. As you perfect the "active listening" method, in which you basically repeat back what a child is saying to you in a way that encourages him or her to go on, you will have the best opportunity of all to improve "both sides" of the communication skill. After all, communication involves two things—receiving or taking *in,* and transmitting or giving *out.* Make it a point this month to listen intently, then to refine what you hear and repeat it back more clearly and more articulately than you heard it.

Example: Your daughter says, "School was the pits today. Nothing but a lot of busywork—stuff the teachers give you to take up the time so they don't have to teach." You say, "The thing you're upset about is that you get assignments that take a lot of time without teaching you very much. And you feel that the *teachers* are being a bit lazy to do that rather than develop ways to challenge you and get you to think."

As you practice this "listen hard and repeat it better" technique, three things will happen: (a) Your children will notice and appreciate the effort you are making to understand them; (b) they will correct you and restate what they mean if your interpretation is incorrect; and (c) over time they will start saying what they mean more precisely so that you will have less chance of misinterpreting them.

4. Stranger conversion. In almost every facet of our lives and daily activities, there are people with whom we rub shoulders and whom we ought to know, but who remain strangers because neither we nor they take the initiative to convert each other from a stranger to an acquaintance. Sometimes it's other parents we see at PTA or at school, or people who work in our building or ride in the same elevator with, or parents of other children on the Little League team.

Part of good communication is the ability to meet such people graciously and pleasantly. Form the habit of introducing yourself, or asking a question or two that gives others an identity in your mind. Seek and find things you have in common that can serve as the basis for a friendship.

5. Name, face, interest-point remembering technique. All of us admire people who are good at remembering names and faces. We especially admire such people when they remember *us*.

The ability to recall names and facts about people is an important part of communication ability, and it increases our opportunities to communicate effectively with more people. There is a simple three-step process that can make you remarkably good at this rather unusual skills. (This is an expansion of the basic "name remembering" technique mentioned in Month 2.)

1. When you meet someone, *use* his or her name at least three times during that initial meeting. (Repeat it as it is given to you, use it at least once in conversation, and then use it again as you say, "Nice meeting you, _____."

2. As quickly as possible after parting company, write down the person's name (in your date book, on your daily planner) along with some physical char-

acteristics of the person that you noticed. Also write at least one thing you learned about the person in your meeting, preferably something you have in common or that is personally interesting to you. This takes only a few seconds and can be brief enough to fit on one small line, such as "Walter Saunders/bulbous nose/daughter in Saydi's class."

3. Glance at your notes that evening or next morning. As mentioned earlier, memory experts tell us that if we review some fact we have learned within twelve to twenty-four hours after learning it, we can set it in our memory.

6. *Your own methods.* Think for a moment about any other ideas you may have for improving your ability to express yourself. List your ideas here:

Exercises to Teach Children

1. First-Sunday discussion. This activity is intended to make children aware of the goal for the month ahead of becoming better at communicating what they observe. Start this month with a discussion based on the following:

- Read aloud the television editorial from this chapter's "Illustrations and Stories" section. Ask what it means. Ask if the children agree with it.
- How is our ability to speak and communicate clearly connected to our ability to think? How is it connected to our ability to help others?
- What are some bad habits or patterns of communication that you notice at school (slang, bad sentences, improper English, such as "he goes" instead of "he said," and so on)?
- How does writing help us to think better and speak better?
- What are some ways you can think of that we could communicate better and more fully during the month ahead?

2. Prequiz. Have each family member take the following quiz on the left-hand side of a piece of paper:

- Pick an object in the room and describe it as completely as possible in writing, using as many adjectives as you can.
- Pick another person in the room and describe him or her as completely as possible.
- How many times during the month past did you: (a) write a poem; (b) give a speech; (c) write in your journal; (d) write a letter?

- How many times did you pause and think about just how to say something before you said it?
- How many times did you notice that someone you were talking to didn't really understand what you were saying and therefore you said it again—this time more clearly?
- What's the best way to resolve an argument or dis- agreement?
- How many new words did you learn during the month past?

3. Elimination of TV on weeknights. This will give children more opportunity to communicate and to remove bad models of communication from their consciousness. Perhaps no single act or decision contributes more to both the quality and the quantity of communication in a family than the elimination of television. There is no need here to rehash the well-known statistics about how much time children waste in front of TV sets. Two things, however, are certain: (a) There are very few examples of articulate communication and a lot of examples of shabby English on television; and (b) children don't communicate at all during the big blocks of time they spend watching it. We believe that the most effective and reasonable system is simply to allow *no* TV on week nights. If a VCR recorder is available, special shows can be recorded for watching on weekends.

4. Communication with the written word. Provide vehicles to help children communicate effectively through writing. Pick the methods best suited to your children. Many of these are the same methods used in Month 1, on observing. They are repeated here with the emphasis on communicating. Think of this month as a "second push" to develop writing and written expression skills in your children.

JOURNALS OR DIARIES: Children should be encouraged to write not only about their activities but about their thoughts and observations. Encouragement is the key. Most children enjoy keeping records. If you share your journal with them and praise their efforts, the chances of their enjoying it enough to stick with it are good. Some families find that it is effective to pick one dinner hour each week when family members are asked to share one short reading from their journals for the previous week.

Getting kids committed to writing in journals is not an easy task. Spend one Sunday afternoon reading a few excerpts from your own journal, if you have one, and/or the journals of grandparents or relatives who are important to the children. Try to impress on them the tremendous value that journals have, not only for their own posterity but also for themselves as they raise their own children. Explain that although it may seem impossible to them at present, it is a fact that they will forget most of what is happening to them now. Recording their experiences and feelings will be invaluable later—often funny, always insightful, and a great way to help their own children realize that *they* were once children. Once they have been convinced of the importance of their own personal journals, see that each child (and parent too) has a special place to keep a journal and spend one Sunday afternoon writing in them together. Assign a specific time each Sunday to write, or let the children set their own goals for writing. Our older girls write several times a week, and even though the younger ones don't write very often, what they do write is always very interesting—sometimes hilarious. Sharing things from our own children's journals may be the literary equivalent of showing home movies to strangers, but the following excerpts will suggest how useful journals can be in providing insights into the nature and character of children.

Our son Joshua's entries show how observant he is, especially of certain things. They also show how laconic he is, unless something really unusual happens.

JOSH AT SEVEN: "On Thursday I got a new magic set and caught four lizards out in the rocks."

JOSH AT EIGHT: "We went to a museum and saw early computers."

JOSH AT NINE: "It was an ordinary day *except* that I got a calculator wristwatch."

JOSH AT TEN: "Today we went to the Polynesian Cultural Center. In the Samoan village the guy was supposed to demonstrate coconut-tree climbing. He said, 'Just a minute, let me go get the ladder' (joke). When he was in the tree, he said, 'You can go now, I live here.' When he husked the coconut, he said, 'We call the coconut juice 7UP because it does not have caffeine. Never had it, never will!' When he made a fire, my dad asked him what kind of wood he used. He said, 'Firewood.' All of the other countries were fun too.

"That night was the best. I walked to the main theater, and a Hawaiian lady that used to visit us at home put a beautiful lei on me and kissed me. We went in the theater to watch *This Is Polynesia*. They were the best performers I have ever seen. People from every country performed. The people from Samoa had boards with fire on them. This was the best moment of my life."

JOSH AT TWELVE: "The Apple II computer is now in my room!"

Saydi's journal shows her free spirit, her somewhat scatterbrained nature, and a level of candor that could be trouble. (It also occasionally shows her amazing phonetic spelling—she is intimidated by no word.)

SAYDI AT SEVEN: "Hi there, I'm very happy. But I have bad news. Shawni won't play any more games with me. But I have good news. It is that my mom had a baby boy. Now I'm a *girl,* but I say oh boy!"

SAYDI AT EIGHT: "Dear Jurnel. Hi. I'm happy. Well, really, I am weird. I got a doll for Christmas. Her name is Jingur. She is cute. Very cute. She has dimples. They are what makes her cute. I treet her as a baby and as my sweet heart.

"Right now I'm eating a valentine candy that says 'kiss me' on it, so I guess you can.

"My cousin broke her arm. She was jumping on her mom's bed when CROLOP! she missed and fell on the floor."

SAYDI AT NINE: "Dear Jurnel. Your name is now *Gertrude.* Gertrude, I love you. We went to Mexico two times. Today is a good day. We finished our club house. Oh boy I'm going to be in fourth grade. I feel great because my mom cut my hair a few days ago and it looks real good. Bye bye."

SAYDI AT TEN: "I'm changing your name to Cookie monster. CM for short. Today was exciting. Do you want me to tell you what I did? I got up and cut my bangs by myself, but I cut it too short, but it *still* looks OK. Bye."

SAYDI AT ELEVEN: "Dear CM. I'm skipping lines and drawing big pictures because I don't like this book as well as my new journal. So I have to fill this one up. I'm in the play of *Annie* now. I *am* Annie. Rehersl is fun."

Shawni's diary reveals some of her discipline, her sensitive nature, and how well she deals with her feelings (along with her sense of humor).

SHAWNI AT EIGHT: "Since I'm just starting a journal, I'll write some things I remember from when I was little. One day Saren asked me if I wanted a knot or a bow in my shoe. I said a bow, but Saren said, 'I can't tie a bow, so do you want a knot or a bow.' So I said a knot.

"I was with my cousin Elisha, and her mom said not to pick the flowers. But I did pick them. Elisha said no, but I kept picking them, so she hit me with a book on the head. And I started screaming.

"Really a long time ago, when I was small, Saren tried to stuff my little body in the refrigerator!

"The things I've always not liked the most are eggplant and my sister wiping her hands on my back."

SHAWNI AT NINE: "Well, today I have to work out a plan on how to do more practicing. So here's a chart right in my journal that shows how much I'll practice the piano every day."

SHAWNI AT TEN: "Last night Mom had the baby. When we went to the hospital, no one could hold him yet except Dad. I can't wait to hold that sweet baby in my arms. I just love him so much."

SHAWNI AT ELEVEN: "Your name is Cuthbert (after my rabbit). Dear Cuthbert, my friend and I got in a big fight.

She really wants to be popular, and I guess she doesn't like me because she thinks I'm not popular. She plays with another girl who is kind of mean and stuck up, and now she's getting that way too. I feel sad. But I've got other friends. On my braces, I got headgear and another thing to pull my bottom teeth forward. I have to wear them both at night, and if you add that with my braces, that is a big mouthful."

SHAWNI AT ELEVEN: "The bad thing that happened today was softball. I got two strikes, but then I hit the ball and got to first. Another person hit the ball, and I ran to second, saw that the ball was not caught, and ran for third. Someone yelled that I should go back. I didn't know what was wrong or what to do, but I ran back and got out. I tried to forget it, but I feel so embarrassed."

SHAWNI AT ELEVEN: "Dear Cuthbert. I must tell you that I'm very sorry about what I wrote on May 25. I don't really hate Josh. Its just that Josh made me so mad that day. Saren and I are going to try to be very, very nice to him because we figgure most bad criminals had a bad childhood. Well, I just wanted to apologize."

SHAWNI AT TWELVE: "I've decided that I'd really like to get my ears pierced. The earrings here are so inexpensive that I just keep thinking about having them pierced. I even got some earrings, and Mom said it was OK with her. Dad says that having holes put in your body is dumb, so I'm not sure."

SHAWNI AT TWELVE: "I got my ears pierced. One of them is in the wrong place so I'll probably have to go back and have it pierced again. I'm so mad I didn't tell the lady when it looked like she was doing it in the wrong place."

Saren's writing has always been so articulate that her journal reads like a story—sometimes sad, sometimes happy, usually somewhat romantic, and always descriptive and clear.

SAREN AT TEN: "Yesterday Cabby, sweet little Cabby our puppy died. Some lady wasn't looking where she was going. We were waiting by the bus stop and the front wheel and the back wheel ran over Cabby's sweet little body. It's *so* sad. It makes me cry just to think about it."

SAREN AT ELEVEN: "Everything in Hawaii is so beautiful. Everywhere I look I see coconut trees and palm trees. There are many strange and wonderful birds. Waimea Beach has such huge waves. We just let the water come in and hit us. Sometimes the waves would hit us so strongly that we would fall over and get all sandy, but it was worth it."

SAREN AT TWELVE: "Our house seems messy. I don't know whether I'm just noticing it more or if it's really getting worse. Dad has a plan: Saydi and Josh's room will have only two chairs that fold into beds (1 each). All of their clothes will be put in the laundry room. It will be like a library. They must check in the clothes they are wearing before they take out clothes for the next day (as though their clothes were books)."

SAREN AT THIRTEEN: "Yesterday I had quite a scare. Eli went down and drank some chemical from Josh's microscope set. I was babysitting alone so I called poison control, and they said (after a lot of talking and looking things up) that they would send paramedics. Mom got home while the paramedics were on the way. Four men came in a big red fire truck with flashing lights.

They gave Eli something to make him throw up. He's fine now."

SAREN AT FIFTEEN: "Scrooge is over. I'm so glad. I've loved being in the play. It seems like there's nothing to do anymore. I feel like crying. I miss my Cratchett family. They were like a real family to me. We had so much fun together. Everyone cried on closing night."

SAREN AT SIXTEEN: "Opening night. My first experience as a director. I can hardly believe it came off. There were some rough spots, but for the most part it was really good. The hall was full by 7:15 and people were still pouring in. It was great! I'm so happy!

POETRY: At one point a few years ago we became particularly concerned about how structured and scientific our children's education seemed to be and how little of their day was devoted to any kind of sensitivity or art or personal expression. We were lucky enough to find some other neighborhood parents who felt the same way and to find a poetry teacher who was willing to come once a week for a month to teach a group of children the joy of poetry. We shared some of the results of that class earlier in this book.

In the neighborhood group were several adolescent boys to whom the thought of poetry was somewhere between ridiculous and repulsive. We persuaded them to try it, and the results were remarkable. The teacher explained how "free" poetry could be, how they could write anything they wanted about anything. She pointed out that most things we do are governed by a lot of laws and rules. But in poetry there are no rules. You can even spell and punctuate however you please. She got the children into discussions about favorite sounds and favorite feelings.

Try these explanations and encouragements with your children, but remember that the best way to encourage a child to write a poem is to write one of your own with the child and to let him or her see the enjoyment you feel.

LETTERS: We don't write enough letters in today's society. The phone is easier. And often we don't even call the people we ought to be caring about and staying in touch with, perhaps simply because the phone is there, reassuring us that we could call if we needed to—so we don't.

But letters are not the same as phone calls. Written words can be more carefully crafted and can say more precisely (and often more beautifully) what we wish to say. They can also be read and reread, pondered and thought about and cherished by a grandmother or relative or friend.

Some families we know set aside one evening each month to write letters as a family. They make photocopies of the children's letters before they send them and thus obtain a valuable, sequential record to go along with journals and other family writings.

ANCESTORS' WRITING (JOURNALS OR LETTERS): If you have any old diaries or writings of your parents, grandparents, or other ancestors, be sure to read them to your children. Discuss what they were saying and why they were saying it, and how they expressed it.

READING TOGETHER: Reading aloud is often thought of as something parents should do with small children. But the practice also pays tremendous dividends with adolescents. Reading good literature together opens all kinds of good opportunities for discussion, not only about the subject matter but about the writing itself and about how the author expressed himself or herself, what styles and forms of writing are used, and so forth.

5. Communication with the spoken word. This will naturally provide an additional vehicle to help you and your children improve verbal communication ability.

SPEECHES: As noted in earlier chapters, having to give short, extemporaneous speeches around the dinner table provides excellent training for the ability to think on one's feet and to express oneself clearly.

DEBATES: The ability to take one side of an issue, craft a case for it, and clearly express that case in words is a valuable (and increasingly rare) ability. One way to teach this skill to children is to set up small debates at the dinner table in place of speeches. Think of a debatable topic and assign one child to speak for sixty seconds on the pro side and another on the con. Then give each child a thirty-second rebuttal opportunity. Another chance for debate comes when two children are fighting or arguing. Take the time to sit down with the two of them, formulate *with* them precisely what the disagreement is about, and structure and supervise a debate to solve it. Point out how much more educational and enjoyable a debate is than a fight or argument. You can also set up a debate between yourself and your teenager the next time he or she wants to do something you don't think is advisable. It's a good way to get all the facts and feelings on the table. To understand each other's point of view, trade sides and see if you can debate the other person's position.

DESCRIPTIONS OF INTERESTING THINGS: At the dinner table ask each family member to think back over the day and recall the most interesting thing he or she saw or experienced (as suggested in Month 1). This time, however, ask each person to pause for sixty seconds and think (before speaking) of the most exact way in which to explain his or her "interesting thing."

VOCABULARY WORDS: Try to be aware of useful words that you hear (or use yourself) that would enhance your children's vocabulary. Don't deal much with technical or difficult words, but rather with descriptive, interesting words that children would enjoy learning. Write them down as you become aware of them and invite other family members to do the same. Have a vocabulary list in the kitchen or family room. Use the words yourself and give lavish praise to the children whenever they use them.

THE "WOULD YOU REPHRASE THAT?" TRADITION: Start a tradition in your family of challenging each other to "rephrase" things that are said ambiguously or sloppily. When your son, for example, asks to go over to Johnny's, ask him to rephrase his question, this time telling you why he wants to go, how long he'll be gone, and why he thinks you should let him go. Encourage children to challenge you to "rephrase" so that if you say no, they can ask you to say it again and include why they cannot go, when they might be able to go, and so on.

6. *Bedtime chats.* These will open up an opportunity for some relaxed communication at the end of the day. Many parents find bedtime to be the best moment to open up and talk about what has taken place and been observed that day. Our earliest books, dealing with younger children, recommend that parents tuck their children in as often as possible and ask, "What was your 'happy' today?" and "What was your 'sad'?" With older children the same principle applies.

Sometimes the best way to talk is just to talk! Tell children what is on *your* mind (what you are worried about, what you are excited about). As the trust levels build, they will share their thoughts, too, and respond to your questions.

You obviously shouldn't feel guilty if you can't tuck everyone in every night. Schedules are not that simple. But during this month try to find one or two nights a week when you have the time to spend a few unhurried moments talking to each individual child as you put him or her to bed.

7. *Friend chart and name remembering.* This activity is designed to increase the number of people with whom children communicate. The Friend Chart under Family Focal Points in Month 4 can be reemphasized this month. Try to teach children the same three-point method of remembering names that you are using and encourage them to list the names of new people they have met on the Friend Chart.

8. *Your own methods.* Take a few moments and think about your own children, how good are they as communicators? What things come to mind that would encourage them to speak more precisely, to take more pride in their language, and to want to communicate better? List the ideas you have here:

9. *Postquiz.* On the "first Sunday" that ends this month and begins Month 7, retake the quiz from the beginning of this section. You will be pleased at how much better everyone does at describing things.

Discuss the value of communication. Ask who can think of a habit or tradition you could adopt as a family to continually improve your ability to communicate.

Family Focal Point—"England Nights"

This activity can reward children for their ability to ask questions. During the years we spent in England, in addition to appreciating their superior use of the English language we came to admire (and almost covet) the English system of early bedtimes for younger children. Most English families, partly because of how early it gets dark, feed their young children (those under eight or so) a light dinner called tea when they come home from school and then put them to bed at six-thirty or seven. The parents and older children then enjoy a peaceful "supper" at seven-thirty or eight, often inviting guests to eat with them.

We try, as often as possible, to have what we call an England night, when we put our smaller children to bed a little early and invite someone interesting to eat a later dinner with us and our adolescent children. Guests are selected because they have an expertise that our family is interested in. The dinner provides the children with a unique opportunity to ask questions and be involved in an adult discussion about a specific area. We have had a couple who were experts in American Indian culture, a doctor, a lawyer, a poet, a native of Latin America. We have a list of interest areas that the children have helped create and we watch for acquaintances who could be invited to discuss each topic.

The children know that the key purpose of the occasion is to develop their question-asking and listening abilities. (In fact they know that if they don't do a pretty good job of questioning and participating in the discussion, they will not be invited to the next England night.) They write out a list of questions before a guest arrives so that they will be well prepared to participate in the discussion.

Summary

Communication is the *vehicle* of sensitivity. Through good communication we better understand our own emotions and attitudes. By communicating we learn of the feelings and needs of others. By communicating we are sometimes able to give the encouragement and help that constitute service.

On the first level a good communicator must be able to communicate effectively what he or she sees and observes and must be able to listen well and converse about the observations, perspectives, and expertise of others. That first level of communication has been the subject of this month. Now, in Month 7, we move to the second level, which involves communication of and about feelings. The vocabulary, grammar, and clear thinking we have tried to develop through this month's methods are the foundation for the deeper kinds of communication discussed in the coming month.

Communicating What We Feel

Unexpressed feelings never die; they just get buried and come forth later in uglier forms.

It is difficult to describe or define what an artist is, but a good attempt was made by one who said, "An artist is one who can express feelings in a way that others can understand."

Illustrations and Stories

Unexpressed, uncommunicated feelings are like bottled-up, unused fuel. They never *move* anything, and if they are left too long, they begin either to sour or to lose their potency, or alternatively they blow up.

Enhancing, refining, and recognizing our feelings are good and useful skills, but communication of those feelings is often the actual *transaction* of sensitivity. When we talk about how we feel, we are reaching deeply into our soul. And when these feelings are communicated clearly and effectively, they reach into the soul of the listener.

If feelings could not be communicated, each person would feel only what he or she experienced or what happened directly to him or her. But through the transmission of feelings we can "receive" and actually feel the emotions of the whole range of human observation and experience.

When you stop to think about it, feelings are what all great forms of art seek to communicate. The movies we like most are the ones that make us feel the most. It is the same with graphic art, with music, and with literature.

So even as art is communication, communication is an art—one in which we can train ourselves and improve our abilities.

We suggest that the old cliche "Some things are better left unsaid" may be more true for one whose goal is simply to avoid all conflict than for someone who wants to live fully and appreciate life and other people. As one of the quotes that opened this month reminds us, unexpressed feelings never die; they live on in our subconscious mind and often come forth later in uglier forms. So the other saying might be revised to read, "Don't leave any feelings unsaid, but find the right time and the right way to say them."

I (Richard) have a remarkably clear memory of a particular day in my childhood when I was feeling a special love for my father because of something he had done for me. I was sitting in my bedroom, probably about nine or ten years old, and my father was in the living room reading the newspaper. I wanted to go in, give him a hug, and tell him I loved him. But it was hard to get up and do it. I guess I wondered if I would disturb him. And like many children that age I felt a little embarrassed about expressing a "mushy" feeling.

I remember thinking—analyzing actually—what the pros and cons of the action would be. I finally decided that going out there and telling my dad I loved him really couldn't do any harm and would make him feel happy, and make me feel happy too. I remember making what may have been my earliest mental resolution; it was "When you feel something *good* for people, *tell* them."

An interesting study done among 371 mothers in the 1950s measured and catalogued the parenting methods, techniques, and attitudes employed in each home. Thirty years later interviews were conducted among the adults and parents who had been the children in the homes where the study had been done. They were asked how happy their childhood memories were and how good a parenting job their mothers had done.

The central finding: Good parenting and successful, happy children could not be directly connected to any specific techniques or methods. What they were connected to was how much the mothers had enjoyed their children, how much fun they had had together while the children were growing up, and how much they communicated with each other about their feelings.

I (Linda) have always appreciated our son Josh's particular straightforward way of expressing how he feels. We always know when he is angry because he slams his bedroom door so fast and loud that it sounds like a gunshot. When he was small, he ran away from home quite regularly.

Every once in a while he lets me know how he feels so abruptly that it startles me. It happens when I really bear down on him for a lot of consecutive mistakes. I remember one day, when he was eleven or twelve, when I was really after him.

"Josh, why did you leave your trumpet at school? Why does this room always look like you're having a garage sale? Why don't you take a shower? Why have you lost your homework again?"

Finally he blurted back at me, "Because I'm stupid! I'm just plain dumb!"

In that instant I realized that that was exactly how I was making him feel—like a messed-up, good-for-nothing kid! Believe me, I backpedaled in a hurry and thought of several positive things to say. (It wasn't easy.) Because he is so good at expressing how he feels when his feelings are hurt, I'm often more careful about how I phrase my criticisms—not only to him but to the other children as well!

It has been said that parents would do better if they tried less to make their children good and tried more to make them happy. An extension and corollary to this truth is that parents would also do better if they tried less to communicate *at* their children and more to communicate *with* them—about feelings.

We have a thirteen-year-old daughter who is blessed with an active conscience and an ever-present desire to have everything resolved and straight in her mind. Two or three times a month she comes to one of us and with a little self-conscious half smile says, "I've got a problem. Could we talk?" If only all of our kids did this!

We find some privacy, and she begins. She usually begins with the words "I feel." What follows is always beautiful because it's always honest. And whether or not she learns anything from our advice, *we* learn from her sincerity and her openness.

A neighborhood group held a most interesting social event not long ago. It was a dinner to which only adolescents (ages ten to fourteen in this case) and the most elderly members of the neighborhood were invited. The seating arrangement mixed the oldsters and the youngsters. The resulting conversations were remarkable. At most tables discussions were still going on over an hour after dessert had been served. Each age was completely fascinating to the other. Questions were flying a mile a minute.

Anyone who listened carefully quickly realized that the real conversation was about feelings—how it feels to be old, how it feels to be young, how it feels to share with each other.

Some marriage partners choose to share only a part of each other, to communicate only a portion of their feelings. The relationship could be diagrammed like this ⊙. The overlap, or shared portion, is shaped like a football, and like the bounce of a football, the marriage is erratic and unpredictable. You never know if it will go to you or to the side or over your head.

In a marriage where virtually all is shared, the diagram looks like this ⊙. The marriage (the overlap) is round, like a basketball. Its bounce is straight and true.

Communication about feelings is not only the tool that allows us to serve others, it is often the service itself. For the needs of many do not involve material or physical help, but emotional and social help—which are given with *words*.

It is a skill, and it takes time and effort to learn, but we can teach ourselves first to communicate accurately about personal feelings, then to communicate about the feelings of the person with whom we are talking, and finally to communicate about the probable feelings of people we have observed but never met. To communicate about feelings is to understand those feelings—and to fully comprehend what they mean. There is only one way to form a true relationship: It is to share and communicate feelings.

Approaches for Parents

1. Observe and describe yourself. It has been said that observation takes place on three levels. First we learn how to observe nature and things. Second we learn how to observe other people. Third we learn how to observe ourselves.

As we learn to watch ourselves, it is very useful to attempt to describe what we see. This month, in a journal, diary, or notebook reserved for this purpose, try to write about the moods and feelings you have experienced during the day. Describe how you felt and why you felt that way.

We don't do as well personally with our journals as we wish we did, but when we do write, it is both useful and satisfying. For this chapter we each opened our journals at random to pull out an example (we've been trying for some time to make our journals primarily about feelings). These pages are not literary masterpieces, but they do illustrate the point. Richard's excerpt is first, then Linda's:

> Gloomy day—cloudy and dark. Had to get Shawni admitted in new school. Saw it as a task rather than an opportunity. The admittance officer was blunt, almost rude. That along with the dark day put me in a somber, almost sullen mood. I felt like going back home to bed. It was an hour until the district head would be back (whom I was told I would have to see. Red tape—miles of it).
>
> I used the time to call Craig—just because we hadn't spoken since he changed jobs. I decided to be upbeat in case he needed some encouragement. We had a great chat—changed my mood completely. I went back to the district office, had a time talking to the district head (who

was much more pleasant than the other officer—probably because I approached him in a better way).

I enjoyed the rain on the way back. I've always liked rainy days actually.

Well, here we are—on the last leg of our flight home from Israel—with feet swelling and hearts too and with the prospect of throwing our arms around our priceless treasures—the children.

Rick and I have been grouchy with each other the past couple of days because we miss the kids so much! Absence makes the heart grow fonder, and as we have never left them this long before, we are excited beyond words to squeeze them and love them and teach them again.

Even though the long, squashed plane ride with smokers on every side, long walks up and down the aisles, sweltering and freezing, and sitting for long periods have been difficult (only seven weeks to my due date), none of it has been as hard as it is to be at home—to clean and cook, run errands and haul groceries and laundry and referee arguments. Yet I don't think I could stand one more day of this relative ease, having three meals a day presented to me, only getting one person ready each morning and never having to tie one double knot on anybody's tennis shoes for fifteen whole days. I'm so ready to go back! To breathe a big sigh full of love and determination and get back to "the real thing."

It is through describing our feelings that we understand and control them. Describing feelings somehow captures them and removes the worry from them, rendering them helpless to hurt us.

2. *As you continue the habit of asking "How do you feel?" make it a specific rather than a general question.* During this month, as you did in Month 3, keep aware of

how often you can ask someone how he or she feels. But like the man described in the opening part of Month 2, add some "following" words to make it the kind of specific question that solicits a serious and specific answer. Say, "How do you feel about the decision your boss made?" or "How do you feel when your math teacher calls on you in class?" or "How did you feel right after the cheerleader tryouts?" or "How do you feel at five o'clock on Friday when the weekend begins?"

3. *Form the parallel habit of telling others how you feel.* As we have mentioned, the words *I feel* have a way of opening up a high trust level in a conversation. They also allow their user to say what is in his or her heart without judging or offending the other person. Refocus this month on saying how you feel, and be as clear and articulate as you possibly can about those feelings. For example, if you are upset with your thirteen-year-old daughter for not letting you know where she was after school, your impulse might be to say, "You are irresponsible when you don't ask and you'd better not let it happen again." A more effective, less judgmental (and perhaps more accurate) thing to say would be, "I feel upset and worried when I have no idea where you are."

The first response breeds defensiveness and resentment in the daughter and minimizes her inclination to apologize and try hard not to do it again. The second response breeds concern and maximizes her inclination to apologize and improve of her own initiative.

4. *Discover real feelings instead of scheming to overcome undesirable actions.* Sometimes our biggest problem in dealing with children is that we forget to communicate, focusing instead on trying to manipulate behavior.

When one of our daughters started junior high school,

her biggest problem (in our minds) was that she kept missing the bus. She had done this occasionally in elementary school, but it was getting worse!

This is ridiculous! I (Linda) thought to myself. My morning is timed to the very minute to get everybody to finish their practicing, get their rooms straight, beds made, homework packed up, notes written, and out the door! I just don't have time to drop everything and run her down to the school twice a week when a bus stops for her right outside our door!

My first plan of attack was to tell her that if she missed the bus again, she would just have to be late for school. I thought she would be mortified. I thought it would be agony for her to enter the classroom late—but as it turned out, she didn't say a thing, just got out of the car with her home excuse, said "Thanks," and meandered on in.

The next time it happened (a few days later), I said, "You know, I just can't get you down here today. You'll just have to miss school!" (*Surely that will get her,* I thought. *She's such a good student and it will be difficult for her to make things up!*) Foiled again! She seemed perfectly happy to stay home.

The next time it happened (a few days later), I just tried getting good and mad. "How can you keep doing this to me?" I demanded. "I've had it! You just get your things together and get out that door on time from now on." The tirade had little effect.

The next time it happened (a few days later), I decided to hit her where it really hurt—the pocketbook! "Okay, two dollars every time I have to take you to school from now on," I announced. "That way everybody will be happier." (At least she'll be giving me something for my efforts, I thought. That will make her think twice before she tries this again.)

This time she was mad. "This is just ridiculous to have to pay my own mother for a ride to school," she raved. "I can't believe this!" (I loved it; I had finally figured out something that worked!)

I held the line, however, and we were both fuming as I drove her to school. When she got out, she leaned over and said with a scowl, "Taxi drivers don't deserve thanks!" and slammed the door.

I was stunned. I couldn't believe she could think of something so . . . clever to say to me! I immediately flung the door back open and told her to get back in! We had some talking to do!

In the course of our talk I discovered what had really been happening. We had not been communicating our true feelings to each other. I had been trying to manipulate her behavior, not telling her how I felt. She hadn't been communicating with me either. I found that she hated going to school! She felt as though she was doing busywork in many classes, and most of all she felt desperately alone at lunchtime with no one to eat with or talk to. We spent a good long time *really* communicating—being amazed at how each other felt.

How scary, I thought later that afternoon as I contemplated what had happened and how easily I could have let our communication skills drift farther and farther apart and chalk it up to rebellion or insensitivity. When we finally sat down and really talked, we discovered that the basic problem was self-centeredness on both our parts (yes, me, too . . . I was saying, "How can you do this to *me*?") What we needed to work on was feeling *with* each other and keeping the communication lines open. I don't remember her missing the bus again, except on rare occasions.

5. *Tell others how you think they feel.* Somewhere beyond the habits of asking how others feel and telling them how you feel lies the art of being able to tell others how *they* feel. As a person masters the skill of face reading (from Month 5), he or she becomes capable of giving a very valuable gift to those with whom he or she deals. The person can say, "You look like you're feeling a lot of pressure," or "You sound like you're even more excited about that than you're letting on," or "I appreciate your saying that, but I sense that you still don't feel right about it."

As we make these kinds of statements to people, we are talking to them about their feelings, and they will respond—either to agree with our assessment, to disagree with it, or to expand or alter it. In every case windows will be opened to us that allow us to see feelings and to notice opportunities to give encouragement or help that is tailor-made to the feelings and needs of the other person.

6. *Give the incredible gift of a well-conceived compliment.* Some of the most vivid and valued childhood memories are of simple compliments. I (Richard) remember a hunting trip when my father told me how much fun I was to have along and how sharp my eyes were at picking up distant movement. I remember my mother praising specific grades on a report card and asking me where I had obtained my aptitude for math, since I couldn't have gotten it from her. And I remember a little sixth-grade girl who coyly told me what a good dancer I was and with that one simple sentence drastically changed how I viewed several things, including dancing.

Just as the body needs physical nourishment, the human ego needs the nutrients of praise. And the fast food of a "Good game" or a "You look nice" will not mean as much as a carefully prepared gourmet compliment such as "You did an exceptional job on that model. You've always been really talented with your hands, and the way you painted it shows you have a real 'feel' for color and design," or "I was noticing you with your friends after Sunday school and you really have a way of keeping everyone involved and including all the other kids in the conversation. I could tell by watching how much they like and respect you."

When you give a compliment: (a) be sure it is completely honest; (b) make it as specific as possible; and (c) get as much eye contact as possible with the person so you can say it with your eyes as well as with your voice.

Children, particularly adolescents, thrive on praise and use it as fuel for their flame of self-esteem. Parents who consciously strive to communicate as many of the positive feelings and as much of their pride as possible find their children to be happier and more manageable.

Criticism is simply not an effective teaching method. When it is used at all, it should be focused on an action, not on a person, and it should be "sandwiched" between layers of praise.

7. Orient personal conversations toward feelings. In addition to talking about how you feel, and how the person you are speaking with feels, it is possible in everyday conversation to turn discussions about third parties toward feelings. Doing so elevates a conversation and helps avoid gossip.

For example your friend says, "Did you hear that since Fred lost his job, he and Mary are considering separation or divorce?" Rather than following the typical pattern of gossip, you say, "I wonder what feelings Fred had to deal with in being laid off. Probably felt some bitterness and maybe some insecurity. What do you think?"

By shifting the conversation to feelings, you end up empathizing rather than gossiping.

8. *Be honest.* Nothing promotes meaningful communication more than candor and honesty. Honesty and openness are very disarming; they take down the other person's defenses and encourage him or her to talk and respond to you in a way that is equally honest and thus very revealing of his or her truest and innermost feelings.

Complete honesty means not exaggerating; it means saying what you really think rather than what's expected. And it means taking down facades and artificial images.

It is not easy, but it is rewarding. Commit yourself to total candor for this month and you will be amazed at the growing sense of power and inner strength that results.

9. *Your own methods.* List any other ideas that come to mind, ways you could improve yourself and concentrate more on the skill of communicating about your feelings and about the feelings of others:

Exercises to Teach Children

1. First-Sunday discussion. This is to help children understand this month's goal of communicating effectively about *feelings.*

- Last month we talked about and worked on being able to describe and communicate the things we see or observe. This month we work on communicating feelings. Why is it important to communicate about feelings? (Read the "unexpressed-feelings" quote that opens this chapter and discuss.)
- *When* do we need to be able to talk about feelings? (When we're upset, when we disagree with someone, when our own feelings are hurt, when we are happy, when we want to make someone else happy, and so on.) At this point in our family discussion our ten-year-old revealed that her favorite song from when she was little was one by Marlo Thomas that goes "It's all right to cry, crying gets the sad out of you." She said the song always made her feel good. How can talking about feelings help other people? (By letting them know they are understood. By revealing ways in which we can help them.)

2. Prequiz. Answer the following:

- How many times during the past month have you talked with someone about your feelings or about theirs?

- How many times have you written about your feelings (in your journal, in poetry, or such)?
- How many specific compliments can you remember giving to other people during the past month?
- Write down the best compliment you can think of right now for some other member of your family.
- Based on what you can see right now and on what you've noticed lately, write a short paragraph about how you think some other family member is feeling at this moment.

3. Provide an example. This is intended to give children a communication model to follow. It goes without saying that kids will begin to communicate feelings as they see and hear you doing so. Talk openly about your moods and feelings and ask often about theirs. You will thus teach your children two profoundly important principles: (a) It is okay to have feelings—the whole gamut of feelings; and (b) it's healthy and beneficial to express those feelings (in the proper place and at the right time, but soon, before they fester or come out in other ways).

4. Adding feelings to activate listening. This will encourage and draw out children's feelings in conversation. The active listening discussed in Months 2 and 6 reaches its highest form when it centers on feelings.

Listen carefully to what a child is saying, rephrase it, and then add an assessment or supposition about how that thing must make the child feel. For example: "I see what you mean, John. Your coach tells you to do it one way, but then he praises Billy, who's doing it a different way. That's got to be a little frustrating for you because you're the one trying to follow the directions, but you're not getting the praise. I think if I were you, I'd feel pretty confused about just what to do next."

5. Bedtime chats. We noted in the preceding month what a good moment bedtime can be for communication, and we mentioned various fun questions to ask children at bedtime. Try during the month to expand this idea a little so that it includes the expression of more specific feelings.

Start it off yourself by sitting on the edge of a child's bed and volunteering how you have felt about various things during the day. Let the child respond in kind. Prompt him or her along with questions, encouragement, compliments.

Don't expect feelings to flow as freely as you wish on the first few efforts. Be content to talk about your own feelings a few times and be patient about your children's expressions.

6. *Writing and reading about feelings.* Here we use methods from earlier chapters in new ways to help children better define and articulate their feelings.

- *Themes.* Write a list of feeling-describing adjectives on a blackboard or chart (*enthusiastic, somber, jealous, ecstatic, frustrated, embarrassed*) and ask each child to write a one-page theme on "One time when I felt _____." Encourage a description of the feeling as well as of the circumstances.
- *Journals.* Ask all family members to concentrate this month on writing about feelings in their journal entries—both their feelings and the feelings they perceive others to have.
- *Magazine-picture-game* (an adaptation of a method from Month 5). Select a few pictures from magazine ads that contain a central person or group. Point to a person in a picture, invite the children to study his

or her environment and circumstances and then to begin stating adjectives that might express what the person is feeling. Keep a list of all the adjectives mentioned.

- *Ancestor records or journals.* If you have the diaries or records of grandparents or ancestors, locate passages that either describe feelings they experienced or situations in which you can imagine or speculate how they felt. Read them along with your children at dinnertime.

- *Adjective lists of feelings.* Build and expand your previous lists to help children realize how many moods, emotions, and feelings exist and how interesting they are to experience. Take the list started in the magazine-picture game or used in writing themes and expand it in a family discussion. As the list grows, explain that as we develop and mature, we experience an increasingly wider range of feelings and emotions. Use the metaphor of an explorer who discovers new continents, new rivers, previously unknown mountain ranges, and the like. Just as bold and successful explorers were unafraid of challenging new territory, so we should be unafraid and unashamed of acknowledging and expressing our feelings.

7. *Feelings "clearinghouse."* This exercise is designed to assist children in having a vocabulary to explain their feelings and to realize the advantages of expressing feelings rather than holding them in. During the month find some opportunities to "clear away" any unexpressed feelings that any family member has. Using the adjective list, go through it together, and say, "Has anyone been feeling

frustrated? Jealous? Angry?" and so on right through the list.

Preface the clearinghouse by quoting the phrase "Unexpressed feelings never die; they simply get buried and come forth later in uglier forms."

Be sure children understand that this is just an exercise to help them identify feelings and to show them how much better they feel after honest emotions are expressed. Remind them that there will usually not be this kind of game to provide a way to express how they feel; thus they should, on their own, think about how they feel and share those feelings with other family members.

8. *One-on-one opportunities.* This is intended to facilitate the most personal expressions of feelings, one-on-one, between parent and child. Take a child on routine travel whenever possible. Whether on a business trip or a simple visit to the grocery store, try to take a child along. One-on-one situations facilitate communication of feelings more effectively than any other setting.

A trip, whether across country or across town, is a particularly effective vehicle for communication. Since you are on your way somewhere, you feel no pressure to be doing something. You can talk, because there is essentially nothing else to do until you reach the destination. This relaxed atmosphere of time availability leads to easy and pleasant communication.

9. *Your own methods.* List here any other ways you can think of to help children become better at explaining and communicating about feelings:

10. *Postquiz.* Retake the test from the beginning of the chapter. You will find that the questions are easy this time rather than perplexing. Praise the children's improvement.

Family Focal Point—The Comp Award

The *Comp Award* will keep children aware of trying not only to know how others are feeling but to help them feel better by communicating their own positive feelings.

Remember the Icebreaker Award in Month 2? We have found that a brief award ceremony each Sunday at the dinner table is an exciting and effective way to extend praise and recognition to children. At first we were concerned that teenagers would think they were a little above this type of activity. On the contrary, we found that they want (and need) recognition as much as or more than the smaller children and always want to be in the running for the awards we give.

This month we suggest the Comp Award. In our family it came about this way: Grandma was visiting us and was involved with us one evening as we discussed this month's goal of trying to know how others are feeling. She told us of a teacher she once had, long ago when she was a little girl. This teacher, she said, had a gift for knowing how children felt and for offering words of encouragement or praise when they were needing them most. Grandma said she remembered how this teacher would come up to her and say, "I have a comp for you. It's a good one, and I'll give it to you after school." Grandma would then feel happy and excited all day, waiting to see what nice thing the teacher would say to her.

With Grandma's story in our minds we discussed how powerful a good compliment can be. We talked about how a person has to observe and listen and try to know how the other person is feeling before he or she can give a good and thoughtful compliment. And we talked about a good compliment as the highest form of "feelings communication."

We decided it was something important enough that we should remind ourselves of it each week. So we established the Comp Award. It consists of a piece of construction paper with a carefully lettered COMP mounted on cardboard.

Each Sunday at dinner we ask, "Who's in the running?" and the children think back, trying to recall any instance during the past week when they noticed enough about another person and sensed his or her feelings well enough to communicate a good compliment.

The children listen to each other's experiences in giving compliments and become more motivated to give better compliments themselves. The Comp Award is presented to the person who gave the best compliment. He or she keeps the award on his or her bedroom door throughout the week until next Sunday, when it is reawarded.

Summary

The ability to communicate feelings accurately and honestly is an essential part of charity. We must know of the feelings of others in order to serve them, and we often serve them best simply by expressing our feelings to them and for them.

This month's exercises and approaches attempt to help children and parents to sort out and better define our feelings as we talk about them and to better grasp the feelings of others as we listen to them. It is important to remember that the efforts we make to communicate what we feel actually expand and extend the range of what we feel. The extra thought that it takes to articulate our emotions serves to enhance those feelings and to complete them.

Doing

All of the observing, listening, feeling, and communicating skills we have tried to develop in ourselves and in our children over the past seven months come into their full fruition when they bring about the action of service.

Writer and philosopher James Russell Lowell said, "All the beautiful sentiments in the world weigh less than a single lonely action."

English author William R. Inge said, "Beautiful thoughts hardly bring us to God until they are acted upon. No one can have a true idea of right until he does it."

Ralph Waldo Emerson said, "Man's actions are the picture book of his creeds."

John D. Rockefeller said, "I believe that the rendering of service is the common duty of mankind and that only in the purifying of sacrifice is the dross of selfishness consumed and the greatness of the human soul set free."

Francis Bacon perhaps said it best of all: "*All our actions take their hue from the complexion of the heart, as landscapes their variety from light.*"

UNDERSTANDING

OBSERVING

FEELING

COMMUNICATING

+DOING

_____

=SENSITIVITY

Service

You will find as you look back upon your life, that the moments that stand out are the moments when you have done things for others.

—HENRY DRUMMOND

True generosity requires more of us than kindly impulse. Above all it requires imagination.

—I. A. R. WYLIE

Illustrations and Stories

One snowy December night in a poor part of London, we took our four small children on a mission of service. Our destination was an orphanage, populated mainly by retarded children. Each of our children had decided the previous night in a family meeting to choose one of their best toys to give to one of the orphans. We had called the orphanage to make arrangements and to get the names of four children whose ages corresponded with those of our kids.

That evening lives as a vivid memory in the now much older minds of our children. They remember the huge old

Victorian building that housed the orphanage. They remember the looks of pleasure on the small orphans' faces. They remember a little girl named Rebecca, who took little interest in the doll she was given but *loved* the tiny doll dish and spoon that went with it. Most of all they remember the warmth and light they felt in their hearts on that cold, dark night. They know it for what it was—the light of giving, the warmth of service.

I (Richard) observed a young neighbor boy across the street. I watched him from my window one snowy Saturday morning, hearing nothing but seeing enough to tell a beautiful story. He skipped out of his front door into the bright, white winter Saturday, basketball under his arm, sneakers on his feet, smile on his face. He trotted down his walk, dribbling the ball and making a head fake or two wherever there was a dry patch of pavement on the carefully shoveled sidewalk.

I had noticed the same boy doing the snow shoveling earlier that morning as I went out to pick up the morning paper.

Now he turned onto the main sidewalk and loped past his neighbor's house. Then he paused, looked back, hesitated, started running again, stopped again. He was looking at the old lady who lived next door in the house he had just passed. She was struggling with a heavy old snow shovel. Again the boy started down the street. Again he paused. I could see his thoughts as clearly as if I were inside his head: *The guys are waiting for me. I'll miss part of the game. I've already shoveled snow this morning. But she can't do it. She's too frail. She might hurt herself.*

He tossed the ball into a fluffy snowdrift and ran back to get his shovel. The look on his face was an interesting combination of exasperation at the situation and satisfaction in having decided something he knew was right.

It has become a tradition in our family to stop and help whenever we can. We don't pick up every hitchhiker we see, but when we spot one who looks to be in real need, we stop. One raw winter day we rounded a bend in the road and confronted a hitchhiker, old, tattered, probably cold. Our whole family was in the van. We were crowded and late getting home. But we stopped, drove him into town, talked and made friends all the way, found him a motel room, and paid for it.

As we drove home, there was a quiet, peaceful feeling in the van, a rare moment of real silence. It was broken by our seven-year-old, who said, "Dad, now I understand about the Good Samaritan."

Teddy Roosevelt said, "In the battle of life, it is not the critic who counts. Not the man who points out where the strong man stumbled or where the doer of the deeds could have done better. The credit belongs to the man who is actually *in* the arena . . . who does actually strive to *do* the deeds . . . whose place will never be among those cold and timid souls who never knew either victory or defeat!"

Tennyson said (as we have all heard), "'Tis better to have loved and lost than never to have loved at all."

What really puts us in the arena? What really lets us

undertake the risk of actively loving? The answer is service.

Those who serve are involved. They are no longer mere spectators of life. And they will never be among the "timid souls," who rarely lose and rarely win.

"I think we need to go and see Mr. Boyle," twelve-year-old Joshua said one day out of the clear blue.

"I think so too," I said, "but what made you think of that?"

"Well, tonight some of the Scouts were talking about an old man who the police found in his back bedroom just staring at the wall. He was weak and sick and lonely and had apparently not moved from the bed for several days."

Mr. Boyle was a family friend, actually assigned to us at our request by the Community Services Council, which attempts to find help for lonely senior citizens. He was an eighty-seven-year-old widower who had never had children. He had been the youngest child of a family of ten, and his only living relative was a nephew who was two years older than he.

We had taken the children to see him about once a month to cut his grass and plant flowers, pick apples, and listen to stories, but we hadn't been there lately. Josh, in fact, up to this point had been one of the complainers when it was time to go. It wasn't that he didn't want to go; it was just that he could think of more interesting things to do. But something about the story at the Scout meeting had really touched him. We went the next day to see Mr. Boyle, and Josh's usual stoic reserve around adults of any kind melted into a real interest in this dear old man's stories. Josh mowed the lawn and cheerfully worked with his brothers to trim the bushes.

Even his oldest sister, who often acts like she doesn't have much use for Josh, noticed his kindness and said, "You know, if we could get Josh to clean his room as well as he did that yard, I could learn to like that kid!"

Approaches for Parents

1. Attitude. Most service is an outgrowth of attitude. There are a couple of perspectives that make service easier and more natural:

REALIZING THE HONOR OF SERVING CHILDREN: I (Richard) got up six times with our sick eighteen-month-old son one night. Fortunately I had been reflecting earlier that day on what an honor it is to serve children. They are after all the greatest joy of our lives, as well as the most important responsibility we have. No other privilege compares with serving children, and nothing teaches us more. They are really our brothers and sisters more than our children—we all came from the same place, we are all children of God. The presence of this attitude in my mind (although it's hard for me to believe even as I write) actually made it pleasant to be awakened six times in one night and to be given six chances to serve a tiny brother.

WANTING OTHERS' PROBLEMS TO BECOME OUR OWN: All parents have experienced the desire to take pain or sickness away from their children and take it upon themselves. As we learn to love others, it is possible to develop similar feelings for them, and these feelings lead inevitably to service.

2. *Mental effort.* The most effective and useful types of service come in the form of response to need. When we think hard enough to define a need clearly, and then think again, hard enough to find a real solution that we can provide to that need, we become capable of providing true service.

This application of mental effort is sometimes the only way to develop solutions for our children's problems. To illustrate: We remember one period when we felt some rather deep concern about problems that two of our children were having. One adolescent daughter, just starting a new school, felt that she had no close friends and was just too shy to go out and get some. And our preadolescent boy, totally secure socially and with his friends, was performing far below his potential academically at school.

Both problems seemed to drag on and on, and steadily worsened. We worried about them but didn't know just what to do. We kept telling each other that these were just passing phases, and we tried not to think about them.

One day it occurred to us that these problems weren't solving themselves and that we had to analyze them to the same depth and with the same degree (or intensity) of mental effort that we might put into a business or professional problem.

Hard thought led to specific ideas. We mentioned earlier in the book that we ended up throwing a surprise party for our daughter, an overnight slumber party that gave her the time she needed with some other girls to start some new friendships.

With our son, we first spoke on the phone to his teacher and then went to school with him early one morning and met together with him and his teacher. The boy came away with a clearer idea of what he had to do to get better grades, and we gained a clearer understanding of how to help him.

These were not particularly unique or creative ideas, but they worked. The point is that parents can best serve their children when they take the time to think, to use mental effort in deciding what the needs are and just how the needs can be met.

3. Inventory. As simple as it sounds, rendering small acts of service is often just a matter of habit. We do what we condition ourselves to do. And although routine, mechanical service is inferior to thoughtful, heartfelt service, there is still much benefit in becoming consistent and regular in our efforts to serve.

Try this: In your planner, calendar book, or diary draw a small box on each day or date. Then, as you watch for and perform some small act of service, write what it was in that day's box ("Helped Lillian unload groceries," "Took over car pool for Margaret," "Stopped to help elderly man change tire").

A day never passes without little chances to give some kind of service. The only uncertainty is whether you will see those chances. The fill-in-the-box method increases the odds that you will.

4. Wise service. We should all strive to give others, particularly our children, what they need rather than what they want. Usually we can discern the difference between the two simply by asking ourselves objectively what the consequences will be.

All of the skills worked on in the earlier months of this book essentially help us to observe and understand enough to serve the real needs of others. Serving needs rather than wants is what separates true sensitivity from mere "nice gestures."

Sometimes it is *your* wants that get in the way of others' needs. Are you buying the overpriced toy in the airport shop because your daughter needs it, will benefit from it, or will be reassured of your love by receiving it, or are you buying it because *you* want to ease the guilt you feel for not spending much time with her lately? What does your daughter *need* from you?

5. Volunteer. Call your local volunteer office and get involved in some form of voluntary service!

6. Your own methods. Before going on to the ideas for children, take a moment to list any other ways you can think of to give yourself additional ideas and motivation for the giving of service:

Exercises to Teach Children

1. First-Sunday discussion. This activity is aimed at helping children to understand how the skills of the preceding months lead up to service, and to establish concentration on service as the goal for the month ahead. Build an opening discussion around the following points:

- What are the skills we've worked on over the past seven months?
- How do they make us more capable of giving service?
- Relate the "orphan" story and the "basketball or snow shovel" incident from the "Illustrations and Stories" section and discuss them.
- What does service do for the person giving it?

2. Prequiz. Answer the following:

- How many specific acts of service can you remember giving during the month just passed? How many of those were planned and how many were spur-of-the-moment?
- How many times did you give up something you wanted to do or had planned to do in order to help someone else?
- How many times did you ask someone, "Do you need anything?" or "Can I help you in any way?"
- How many times do you remember consciously looking for specific opportunities to give service?

3. Books and stories that emphasize service. Good stories or everyday illustrations of service can become a vicarious experience for children, in which they feel the joy and light that comes through serving. C. S. Lewis's seven-book series for children, "The Chronicles of Narnia," helps them to understand sacrifice and the principles of good versus evil in a way we have never found elsewhere. For younger children, books such as the "values tales" series or even the Uncle Wiggly stories lead to thoughts of turning the mind from the self to others.

Sometimes the very best illustrations of service (and the most memorable and relevant to children) are stories about grandparents or ancestors in which everyday good deeds or thoughtful acts were performed. Think about it. What incidents can you remember from your own experience and from stories you have heard from your parents or grandparents?

4. *Creating an atmosphere of awareness and service* in order to further encourage children to watch for chances to help.

FAMILY MOTTOS: A family should be an institution in the sense of that word's implications of the qualities of permanence, dependability, and loyalty. One thing all institutions have is traditions, and we have previously mentioned many traditions that relate to service. Other trademarks of a true institution are codes of conduct, slogans, and mottos. Think of a good two- or three-word motto for your family that implies service (for example, "Help others," "Watch for needs," "Service to others"). Repeat the family motto often; start family meetings with it, put it on a plaque in the family room, make a needlepoint of it—do anything that increases the family's awareness and commitment to giving service.

FAMILY FLAG: If you want to go one step farther in the "institutionalizing" process, create a family flag that you can display somewhere in the home and even put on a flagpole on special days. The flag could contain the family name, a family crest, and your service-oriented family motto.

5. *Discussion.* Tell children the two following short stories and hold discussions about them:

> The Jones family located a needy family and decided to help them to have the kind of Christmas they could not afford for themselves. They invited the family for dinner one night and got to know them. Another time they took them all out for pizza and got to know them even better. Then they talked about the family privately and planned exactly what they could do for each child and for the parents to make it the best Christmas they had ever had.
>
> Larry was walking home from school one day when he noticed an elderly man whose car had a flat tire. He helped the man get the jack working and put on the spare tire. Closer to home he passed a neighbor who was trying to hang her wash on a clothesline. The wind came up and scattered sheets and other articles across the lawn. Larry helped her gather them up and then stayed to help her hang the wash on the line.

Discuss the differences in the types of service involved in the two stories. One kind was planned and became better because the Jones family took the time to think carefully about needs. The second kind of service was spontaneous. Needs presented themselves to Larry, and he responded to them.

Ask for other examples of planned service. How do you find opportunities for planned service? What are the rewards? What are some other examples of spontaneous service? How do you find this type of opportunity? What are the enjoyment of spontaneous service?

6. *Looking for needs—doing the deeds*. This exercise is intended to help children see the connections between the listening and observing skills they have been learning and the actual rendering of service. Explain to them that whether service is planned or spontaneous, it has observation as a prerequisite. We cannot "do the deeds" until we "see the needs."

Look for opportunities (dinnertime is usually best) to ask about what needs anyone in the family has observed and about what deeds were done or could have been done to assist those needs.

7. *Service awards*. The Sunday awards discussed in previous months are also effective (especially so) for this month. Have an SS (Spontaneous Service) award that goes to the person who can recall the best act of service performed during the week.

8. *Asking*. This exercise will help children realize that there is another way to discover needs besides observing; it is asking what people need. We once heard a speech by a blind woman in which she said how rare it was (and how pleasant) for someone to simply ask what they could do for her. Much more often, she said, people tried to give her some kind of help she didn't really need, and that embarrassed her. People would help her find something that she took pride in being able to find herself, or take hold of her and help her do something that she had long since learned to do on her own. What she appreciated much more, she told us, was people who didn't assume they knew her needs, but asked.

No matter how good we get at noticing or observing the needs of others, we will never know the specifics of their needs as they do. When it is asked sincerely, the question "What can I do to help you?" is the most effective beginning that service can have.

We have some friends whose teenage boys have made a habit of calling on four or five widows in their neighborhood on a regular basis to ask what they can do for them. The widows know how sincere the boys are and have come to appreciate their visits immensely. They tell the boys the things they really need, perhaps an errand or help with something heavy. And the boys derive great satisfaction from helping.

Families can do this kind of "asking" together. Set aside a Saturday morning. Put on your grubbies or work clothes; go to the homes of some elderly, ill, or otherwise needy neighbors; ask what would help them right then; and spend a few hours doing whatever they need done.

9. Service training. Three kinds of discussions can help children become proficient at thinking of the right kind of service to render in a particular situation:

EXPANDED DINNERTIME DISCUSSIONS: This month, in addition to asking what needs anyone observed, ask, "What did you *do* about them?" And then ask, "What else could have been done?" or "What other approach could have been taken?" Help one another think about the different possibilities for service presented by one particular situation. Children are very good at this kind of brainstorming if you praise every small idea or comment they have.

LARGE AND SMALL ACTS OF SERVICE: Discuss how people often think of service as some big act or gift or sacrifice, when in fact an act of service can sometimes be something as small, easy, and spontaneous as a smile.

Emily Dickinson wrote:

They might not need me but they might.
I'll let my head be just in sight.
A smile as small as mine might be
precisely their necessity.

RETURNING-GIFTS GAME: Play a verbal game in which you present a situation and ask how they would respond: "You're given _____ by _____. What could you give in return?" The goal is to help children realize how much they have been given and develop a thought pattern of wanting to return gifts to the sources. For example: You've been given time, attention, and talent this year by a special piano teacher. You've been given freedom by this country of America. You've been given lots of encouragement by your neighbor. You've been given a healthy body. In each case ask, "What could be given in return?" This discussion works best in a group of two or more children where they can brainstorm or compete in thinking of the kinds of things they could give back (with thoughts that range in magnitude from a letter of appreciation to living a good life).

10. The highest service. This exercise is meant to help children realize that the most lasting and beneficial kind of service is the kind that helps other people to help themselves. Read the following quotes together:

"The highest service we can perform for others is to help them help themselves."

—HORACE MANN

"To lift up a fallen man is good. To help him lift himself up is better."

—ANONYMOUS

Then work together on a list of better forms of service: Instead of giving a poor man a fish, teach him how to fish; instead of giving people food and clothes, help them get a job. Instead of tying children's shoes, teach them how to tie their own.

11. Group service projects. These will give children the experience of working with a large group in performing major service. Church and scouting groups often get involved in service projects of various kinds, but it is those who plan the projects who get the greatest fulfillment.

Try organizing a group service project as a family. Find a need that takes lots of "person power" (cleaning up a property, painting a house) and let your children organize and plan it, ask other families to help, figure out when and how to do it.

12. Your own methods. Sit down for a half hour and think about service. What ideas come to mind? How can you get your children involved in more opportunities for service? What things can you do together? How can you motivate and reward their efforts at serving? Write down your ideas here:

13. *Postquiz*. Take the test once again from the beginning of this month. Many of the questions that were hard to answer (or were answered with a zero) a month ago will be easy (and plentiful) as you retake the test.

Praise the children lavishly for their improvement and their new sense of awareness.

Family Focal Point—Free Daddy or Mommy Dates

All of the family focal points in this book are designed to carry on the principles of the chapter long after the monthly focus has shifted elsewhere. Therefore the focal points have to be things with a certain built-in motivation. We have found that what we call the free Daddy date or free Mommy date works in this kind of self-perpetuating way.

In our family Daddy dates and Mommy dates start when children are young, and they are times when one child goes somewhere alone with Mom or Dad. Because our family is large, these one-on-one times are especially valued by our children. We try to have at least one Daddy date or Mommy date with each child every two months.

The children would rather have a date more often, and there is one way that they can: If they find a service opportunity—something they plan that they and one parent could do for someone—we have promised them that one of us will take them (alone) to perform that service. This is a "free" Daddy or Mommy date that they get in addition to their quota of one every two months.

Don't assume that this is only an idea for young children. Teenagers crave time alone with parents too (although they may not admit it).

The motivation of the opportunity to be alone with one parent adds to a child's interest in looking for and finding opportunities for service.

Summary

All of the previous months in this book are devoted to the development of skills and understanding that would lead to acts of service. This month the objective is to focus on those acts themselves and to make them fun and rewarding enough that children want to continue to look for them and participate in them.

Take the time this month not only to think about and perform acts of service but to reflect on a service you have rendered, to recall how happy it made someone else, and to think back and remember how good it made you feel to do it.

Perhaps the most important thing to remember is that "we love whom we serve." We do not necessarily love those who serve us. We need only to look around our society to dispel this notion. We see how many cynics, dropouts, conceited people, and spoiled children there are who take advantage of, criticize, and even despise their parents, their teachers, and the society that serve them.

But we *do* love those whom we serve. And it follows, very simply and very correctly, that those who love most are those who serve most.

We began this book talking about love as the best motivator for service. We have now gone all the way around the circle and found that service is the best motivator for love.

Service is training in loving.

As we teach our children to serve, we are teaching them to love. As they serve, they are participating in love—actually gaining love and absorbing it as they perform the service. And it is the kind of love that frees them from the unhappy prison of self-centeredness.

Anonymous Service

Let not thy left hand know what thy right hand doeth.

—MATTHEW 6:3

The only people who find happiness are those who seek to serve others and succeed.

—ALBERT SCHWEITZER

Illustrations and Stories

Friends of ours who, like us, have a family tradition of helping a needy family at Christmas decided one year to do so anonymously. They discovered the needs of the family they located by nameless calls to neighbors. They prepared gifts and looked for the things they wanted without telling anyone else what they were doing. They labeled the presents "from your secret friend" or "from Santa." They made a late-night Christmas Eve visit and quietly arranged the wrapped gifts on the porch. Then they all got in the car and parked up the street in dark shadows as the fastest boy pushed the doorbell several times and ran for cover. In silence, from the dark car, the whole family watched as the surprised and delighted needy family came to the door and discovered the Christmas they didn't think they would have.

The Bible tells us that those who gain recognition or admiration for their acts of service already have their reward, whereas those who act anonymously will receive a greater inner reward.

There is an inner feeling—a reward of the spirit—that swells secretly inside whenever we can do something for others that does not directly confer glory on ourselves.

Just before Richard stepped out the door to carry out a two-week research project in the drought-stricken, poverty-ridden country of Mali in Africa, Shawni, our twelve-year-old, pressed fifty dollars—half of all the money she had in the world—into her dad's hand.

"Give this to the special people you find there who really need it," she said.

Tears filled our eyes as we realized that the money she had worked so hard for would be going to those who would never know where the money came from.

"Are you *sure*?" Richard asked.

With a confident nod she said, "I've thought about it for a long time, and I'm sure."

Upon Richard's return it was her eyes that filled with tears as he told her of giving part of the money to the mother of a little child whose pregnant-looking stomach was so full of worms that he could hardly walk; part of it to a boy about her age with leprosy, a boy who was missing the thumb it took to hold the money normally; and part of it to a blind man, who sang an African song of gratitude when the money clinked into his beggar's cup.

As her life proceeds, we're sure Shawni will think of that fifty dollars as one of her best investments.

There are three types of anonymous service. The first type keeps the deed secret from all people except the person for whom the deed is done. The second keeps the deed secret from the person for whom it is done, but not necessarily from others. With the third type no one knows who did the deed except God and the doer. Each of these three kinds of service requires imagination, creativity, and sometimes even a little inclination toward intrigue and covert activity.

Type one is illustrated by a man named Milt, who knew of a friend's need for a second loan to get into the home that he and his family so badly needed. The bank's limits and loan criteria left him short of the required down payment. Milt arranged to lend the balance to his friend, on the strict condition that no one else know of the transaction, and on the secondary condition that the friend, someday when he was able, help someone else on a similar anonymous basis.

Type two is illustrated by twelve-year-old Billy and his dad, who decided it was about time they did something really nice for the Folkers, the elderly couple who had been such good neighbors to them for so long. Mr. Folker still shoveled his walk every time it snowed (which was often in the small Montana town where they lived). Billy and his dad knew that the Folkers usually slept late and that Mr. Folker never did any shoveling until late morning. They decided to get up early every morning there was snow and get his walk and driveway done before he looked outside.

Another illustration of type two is provided by Becky, who noticed that the new girl in school was shy and had no friends. She approached a half dozen of her own friends and told them that she was trying to make the new girl feel comfortable. She asked if they would help by doing the same. She told her friends to keep their discussion secret and simply go a little more out of their way to be friendly and make the new girl feel accepted.

Type three is illustrated by Jane. She was one of many who had tried to help Lilly, a young divorcée with three little children who was trying to keep her family together with no more support than a part-time job and occasional unfulfilled promises by her husband to catch up on the alimony. Lilly had always refused help, saying she had too much pride and she would make it just fine on her own, thank you.

So Jane decided to "go underground." On her own, and always anonymously, she found ways to get extra food and clothing delivered to Lilly. It was always accompanied by some form of note that made it seem like something other than a handout. For example one note said, "Thank you for your patronage over the years. This is a token of our appreciation."

Once, when she knew some unexpected bills had come up, Jane sent a cashier's check with an anonymous note that said, "You won't remember this, but you once waited on me at Spencer's Cafe and took the time to talk with me for a minute. I was seriously depressed that day, and your cheerfulness helped me more than you will ever know. Consider this check a tip with interest added on for four years."

Jane even managed to arrange for a better job to be offered to Lilly. She covered her tracks on everything she did.

Stories like this are rare. They are rare partly because they do not happen as often as they should. But they are also rare because no one ever knows about them.

Another illustration of type three is provided by Sue, an adolescent girl who wanted to do something for a wonderful lady who had been her music teacher for several years. Sue thought about it for quite a while and decided, totally on her own, that what the teacher would enjoy most would be a sincere letter of appreciation that could be interpreted as being from *any* student she had ever had. Sue wrote the letter carefully and included an original poem of gratitude. She typed the letter on plain paper and was careful not to include any clues as to who might have written it. The letter thanked the teacher for "changing her life" and for helping her to develop a talent that would be a joy to her forever.

Approaches for Parents

1. *Think about it.* Although opportunities for anonymous service occur around us all the time, few of us recognize and grasp them unless we have been thinking about service. Start by coming up with someone who you know needs something. Then plan a way to deliver that need with one of the three types of anonymity.

2. *Start a private book of anonymous service.* Sometimes having a private diary of some sort (in which you make notes on things you have done or on plans you have for future service) can serve as a motivation and catalyst to keep you aware and conscious of the goal of providing secret service. If you open the book once a week or so, recording anything you have done or needs you have noticed, the process can become a regular reminder as well as a source of joy and inner satisfaction.

3. Start a partnership service. As important as it is to try to do some acts of service that are known only to yourself, it is also exciting and fulfilling to do some things as a couple, working and planning together to secretly meet a need of someone else.

The best (and most enjoyable and consistent) way to do this is to have, at the first of each month, a short partnership planning meeting in which you review your family goals. Schedule the commitments you have for the month and talk about at least one act of anonymous service that you could perform during the month. You will find that talking about it and planning it together is as much fun as doing it. And you will find that the whole process draws you closer together in a rather unique way.

4. Remember that it is often the small things that count. In the preceding chapter we discussed the small services of a smile or a kind word of encouragement. These are often anonymous acts since they can be aimed at strangers, people whom you have not seen before and are likely not to see again.

During this month try to notice the lonely person, the one who looks discouraged, who is withdrawn or shy, on a train, in a public place, while traveling or walking on a downtown street. Try to catch his or her eye, to smile, to say hello, perhaps to ask a question, stay to talk for a minute, offer some cheer and some conversation.

5. Your own methods. List any other ideas that come to mind, other ways of giving anonymous service, ways of finding people who need help but are too proud to ask. Think also about the anonymous service you could provide as a couple or as a family.

Exercises to Teach Children

1. First-Sunday discussion. This activity is intended to focus family attention on this month's goal of giving anonymous service. Remind the children that this is Month 9 in your family's effort to understand and exercise greater sensitivity. Explain to them that sensitivity reaches its most pure (and often most exciting) level when it leads us to do things secretly for other people. Then engage the family in a discussion along the following lines:

- Why is service more inwardly rewarding when we don't receive any outward reward (not even recognition or appreciation)?
- Discuss the three types of anonymous service noted in the first part of this chapter. Relate the five incidents given as examples and see if the children can tell which type each story illustrates. Also tell the

story of the family giving Christmas gifts secretly to another family.

- Try to come up with an idea for an anonymous act of service that your family can provide.
- Draw family names from a hat to begin secret buddies (see Exercise 3).

2. *Prequiz.* Answer the following:

- How many acts of anonymous service can you remember performing during the month just passed?
- In one minute can you think of someone you could help and of a way of giving that help that would be completely anonymous?
- Why does anonymous service sometimes do more good than the same deeds would if they were not done in secret?

3. *Secret buddies.* This is an exercise to apply and practice simple acts of anonymous service within the family. Children of all ages enjoy the secret-buddies game. Simply put all family names (including parents') in a hat and let each person draw. Three people are enough to play the game. Four or five works even better. If anyone gets his or her own name, they draw again.

The name that each person draws becomes his or her secret buddy for the week ahead, and the object is to try to do as many things as possible for that secret buddy, being careful to leave no clues as to one's identity. The secret services may range from making someone's bed or shining his or her shoes to finding or buying a tool someone needs or leaving a note about the things a person is good at or about why that person is appreciated or loved by his or her secret buddy.

After a week has passed, talk first about whose secret buddy did the most and the best things (without yet revealing who the buddies were). Then see who can guess who his or her secret buddy was—then tell.

4. *Anonymous Service Award*. This activity rewards children for taking the initiative of thinking of and doing anonymous service and makes them increasingly aware of future opportunities. To the Sunday awards discussed in previous months, add this award. Ask, "Who is in the running this week?" and let children think back through the week past and recall any type-two anonymous service (where the person receiving it did not know who gave it). Give the award to whoever can relate the best deed.

Call this award *A.S.* Make it on a mounted piece of paper and let the child who wins it post it on his or her door.

5. *Sponsoring a child in an underdeveloped country*. This gives children the chance to serve others who are both very different and very far away from themselves. Another way to make service essentially anonymous is to give it to people who are too far away or too far removed from you to "pay you back" in any way. Various organizations offer opportunities (for a few dollars per month) to sponsor a child by paying for physical support and often for education.

You can make your support strictly anonymous, receiving information only from the organization and not corresponding directly with the child. But there is so much enjoyment and so much benefit in having your children correspond directly with the child that you may want to settle for semi-anonymous service in this case.

6. *Perspectives on anonymous service*. These stories help children see the connections between integrity, conscience, and anonymous service. In World War II a young pilot named Butch O'Hare was trying to get back to his carrier after his fighter plane had been damaged. His squadron commander had sent him back, feeling that his riddled craft was of little further fighting use and that O'Hare should get it back to the carrier while it would still fly.

Reluctant to leave the mission, O'Hare nonetheless followed orders and headed back toward the carrier. On the way, by chance he intercepted a squadron of Japanese zeros, flying from another angle toward the American carrier, which, without its own planes, would have little defense against them. Despite his crippled plane, O'Hare engaged them in a dogfight and ended up shooting down six of the zeros. Finally, when he had run out of ammunition, he began trying to fly directly into the remaining Japanese planes, hoping to knock at least one more down even though it would cost his own life to do so. The Japanese flight leader, seeing that he was dealing with a mad man, with someone who had no regard for his own life, decided to retreat, and flew off in the other direction. O'Hare had attacked them and was willing to sacrifice himself in the hopes that he could bring down enough of them to save the thousands of men on his carrier.

As it turned out, O'Hare was miraculously able to nurse his battered aircraft back to the carrier, landing it safely on the deck. He became one of the war's most decorated heroes, receiving the rewards and accolades for a heroism that he had not intentionally sought. A few years later the airport in his hometown of Chicago was named O'Hare Field in his honor. It was to become one of the busiest airports in the world.

Another story also concerns Chicago. Al Capone, the most infamous of the 1920s gangsters, was charged with crimes time after time by the law, but he never went to jail largely because of the skill and craftiness of his personal lawyer, who was known as "Easy Eddie."

But as time passed, Eddie began to heed his conscience. He knew of Capone's evil, and he knew the best service that he could give others was to turn in Capone. Eddie eventually went to the FBI and said he had decided to turn state's evidence, to help put Capone into the jail he had kept him out of for so long. The government warned him of what he already knew better than they, namely that though they would try to protect him, his life would be in grave danger.

Eddie replied that he had decided what he wanted the most was to leave his small son a good name. That name, Eddie believed, was more important than the risks and more valuable than the wealth he would have to part with by turning on Capone.

Eddie wanted his service to be anonymous—desperately wanted it—but it could not be so. Capone was put in jail, but not long after, Eddie met with an "accident" and was killed.

Eddie's son, however, did grow up with a good name and with his father's courage and desire to serve others. Eddie's son's name was Butch—Butch O'Hare.

7. *Letting others serve you.* This teaches children that service is a two-way street and that it is often just as important to let others serve you as it is to serve them. Ask your children what they think the phrase "we love whom we serve" means. They will likely give pretty good answers. Then ask, "If we want others to love us, what must

we do?" (Let them serve us.) Since others have a need to serve, sometimes the best way to serve them is to find a way whereby they can serve us. In a little different twist of the word this is a form of anonymous service, since they do not realize _we_ are serving _them_ (our service is hidden— camouflaged beneath the service we are inviting them to give us).

The way to do it is to ask. Ask for advice and for help in areas that those you are asking perceive themselves to be good at. Such a request is a compliment. It makes people feel important and draws them closer to you.

8. Your own ideas. As with each month, you can probably come up with other methods that are even better suited to your own children. Take a few moments and think hard about opportunities for anonymous service. Think of ways your family could secretly help others. Write your ideas here:

9. Postquiz. Retake the test from the beginning of the chapter. Compare the results with those of a month ago. Praise the improvements. Discuss how your family can continue to experience the inner joys of anonymous service.

Family Focal Point—Monthly Family Secret Service

Because children of all ages love being a part of surprises, it is not difficult to get them to be active in the process of designing some kind of secret good deed to do once a month.

In our family, when we first began doing this, the kids responded almost too enthusiastically. Some of their ideas were so elaborately secretive that it made us decide they were either watching too much TV or reading too many mysteries.

One month they decided the family down the street really needed a particular book. They decided to bake a cake—baking the book inside of it—and deliver it secretly to the family. Another month they decided that since they had no living grandfathers, they wanted to find an old man whom they could help and get to know. Through the local Community Services Council we located an elderly man with no family, as mentioned in Month 8. We have since had many memorable moments of service, from mowing his small lawn to simply sitting and listening as he tells of his life. The children often notice something around his house or yard that needs improvement. They do these things quietly and privately.

On months when we plan and carry out a family secret service, we inevitably have a great experience, one in which we learn more than we teach and gain more than we give.

Summary

If the entire process of this book is thought of as an equation, perhaps the product or the result is anonymous service. When children or adults get to the point where they are able to think enough about others to look for and find private acts of service to perform for them, we can be sure that they are worrying far less about the self-centered things that so often occupy the minds of adolescents and teenagers.

Take the opportunity when this ninth month ends to have some kind of review with your children. You might go together to a restaurant or someplace that is special to your family and discuss the previous months. See if they understand how the earlier chapters on seeing and listening tie in to the feelings chapters. See if they can grasp how some of those skills help in our efforts to communicate better with others and to do more for them.

Discuss the prequizzes and postquizzes that they have taken at the start and end of each month and compliment them for their improvements. Remind them of the concept of mirrors and windows, discussed earlier. Ask if they understand that concept any better now after learning the skills of the last nine months.

Finally, discuss repeating each of the months during the coming year. Ask which ones they look forward to most. Review the nine family focal points and see which of them have taken root and become permanent parts of your family's life.

Thank your children for *being* your children, for affording you the greatest of all opportunities for sensitivity, the opportunity of being their parent.

Postscript—HOMEBASE: An International Co-op of Parents

Each of the other three books in this series (*Teaching Your Children Joy, Teaching Your Children Responsibility,* and *Teaching Your Children Values*) has spawned parenting programs and organizations. The groups or programs are called TCJ, TCR, and TCV, respectively. The international co-op that operates these programs is called HOMEBASE and has a membership of over fifty thousand parents spread throughout the world.

TCJ is essentially a do-it-yourself preschool program where parents form neighborhood preschool groups, rotating as teacher and meeting in their own homes two mornings a week. They receive detailed monthly lesson plans, tapes, and newsletters that focus on one type of joy each month and develop young children's social skills, self-esteem, and capacities for happiness.

TCR is a program that assists parents in supplementing the education of their elementary-age children. It takes place two evenings per week around the family dinner table and turns dinnertime into an exciting hour of communication and learning. Parents (through a monthly manual, newsletter, and audiotape) teach one form of responsibility to their children each month. The teaching methods and materials also supplement the children's education through simple exercises and verbal games on communication, creativity, and the type of learning that public schools leave out. It has been said that TCR teaches the "other three Rs" of *responsibility, relationships,* and *right-brain learning.*

Both TCJ and TCR get parents more involved in their children's education, and both make teaching easy, because everything a parent needs (visuals, instructions, questions, and taped segments) are included in the programs. Costs to individual families are very modest, since the programs are run as co-ops with tens of thousands of families sharing the costs.

The third program, *Teaching Children Values* (TCV), is a one-day-a-week Sunday program that uses audiotapes and workbook materials to help a family work on one special value each month. One aspect of *sensitivity* is included in each TCV unit.

Through TCV, parents receive a monthly tape (one side for parents, one side for adolescents) that discusses the skill that is emphasized that month (such as seeing, listening, empathizing) and ties each to a particular *value* for life. Also included each month are printed supplements and a monthly newsletter. The materials expand on the book, giving further examples and illustrations and turning each chapter into a monthly unit.

TCV is preventive medicine for parents who want to give their adolescent children the insights and skills that will help them avoid serious adolescent and teenage problems.

The parents' side of the monthly tape is recorded personally by Linda and Richard Eyre. The adolescents' side is recorded by teenagers.

Use the coupon on the next page to request further information on any of the Eyres' monthly parenting programs. Mail to HOMEBASE, 1615 Foothill Drive, Salt Lake City, Utah 84108 (or phone 801-581-0112). You will receive a *free* catalog and audiotape. Send $5.00 for processing, handling, and postage.

HOMEBASE

. . . . is an international co-op of parents dedicated to making children and family their first priority and to the fostering of traditional values and correct principles in all of our institutions and in society at large.

For preschoolers "TCJ" (Teaching Children Joy) or "Joy Schools" - In-home, do-it-yourself neighborhood preschools focusing on the physical, mental and social "joys" of childhood.

For elementary age children "TCR" (Teaching Children Responsibility) - A program (stories, discussions, music) to conduct around the dinner table that teaches all forms of responsibility and self reliance.

For all ages but particularly adolescents "TCV" (Teaching Children Values) - A once-a-week Sunday program — materials and audio tapes to teach sensitivity, honesty and other values.

For busy parents "LFB" (Lifebalance) - A video and audio tape seminar with fill-in-the blank materials on how to balance family, work and personal needs.

Yes! I am interested in the possibility of membership in HOMEBASE. Please send me further information about:

☐ TCJ ☐ TCV
☐ TCR ☐ LFB

Name _____ Phone _____
                                    area code / number

Address _____
              street

_____
city / state / zip

Index

compliments and, 194–95, 202–4
congruence and, 90, 92, 95, 96,
    102, 106–10, 111, 114–15
in everyday conversations, 195–96
exercises to teach children,
    197–202
family focal point for, 202–4
feelings "clearinghouse" exercise
    and, 200–201
first-Sunday discussion on, 197
honesty in, 196
"How do you feel?" questions and,
    190–91
"I feel" expressions and, 96–97,
    101, 111, 114, 191
illustrations and stories of, 184–88
journal writing and, 189–90, 199
magazine-picture game and,
    199–200
in marriage, 188
one-on-one opportunities for, 201
postquiz on, 202
prequiz on, 197–98
providing example of, 198
trying to manipulate behavior vs.,
    191–94
writing themes in, 199
Comp Award, 202–4
compliments, 128, 194–95, 198
asking for advice or help as, 236
awards for, 202–4
at bedtime, 129
in conversations, 73–74
guidelines for, 195
people put at ease by, 83–84
see also praise
concern, 87, 117–38, 139
approaches for parents, 121–26
argument-ending technique and,
    124–25
children's capability for, 118–19,
    121, 136–37
delaying advice until after expres-
    sion of, 125–26
desire and, 121–22
exercises to teach children, 127–37

family focal point for, 137–38
first-Sunday discussion on, 127–28
illustrations and stories of, 117–21
listen, paraphrase, and add feelings
    game and, 135–36
mental effort required for, 122
one-on-one time with children and,
    124
for oneself vs. others, 122
of parents for children, 122–24
postquiz on, 136–37
prequiz on, 128
question asking and, 131–32
responsibility and, 132–35
role-reversal games and, 130–31
self-esteem and confidence as pre-
    conditions for, 128–29
see also empathy
conflict avoidance, 185
Confucius, 26
congruence, 87, 89–116
adjective game and, 111
and altering of feelings, 97–98
approaches for parents, 95–99
exercises to teach children,
    100–114
expressing feelings and, 90, 92, 95,
    96, 102, 106–10, 111, 114–15
family focal point for, 114–15
family storytelling and, 102–6
first-Sunday discussion on,
    100–101
honesty and, 90, 95
humor and, 110–11
identifying feelings and, 90, 92,
    93–94, 100, 102, 111
"I feel" expressions and, 96–97,
    101, 111, 114
illustrations and stories of, 89–94
journal writing and, 111
less pleasant periods and, 98–99
moving moments and, 99
physical factors and, 112
poetry writing and, 90–91, 106–10
and positive side of negative feel-
    ings, 98–99

INDEX

About the Authors

Linda and Richard Eyre's *Teaching Your Children Values* is the first parenting book to reach the #1 spot on the *New York Times Book Review* bestseller list since Dr. Benjamin Spock's *Baby and Child Care.*

Richard, a Harvard-trained management consultant, and **Linda,** a musician and teacher, have advocated strong families and balanced lifestyles in major national media ranging from "Oprah" and "Donahue" to "The 700 Club" and "Today," and from *The Washington Post* to *USA Today,* as well as through their international parents' cooperative organization, HOMEBASE, and as the hosts of the national cable TV show "Families Are Forever."

Parents of nine children ranging in age from eight to twenty-four, the Eyres live in Salt Lake City and Washington, D.C.